Fifty Lessons

in

Training for Service

by

HERBERT MONINGER, A. M., B. D.

Author of

Standard Commentary on the International Sunday-school
Lessons, Studies in the New Testament Church
Graded Supplemental Lessons,
Timely Suggestion

Revised Edition

For Use in

Teacher-training Classes,
Young People's Societies,
Mid-week Prayer-meetings,
Adult Bible Classes, etc.

════

PUBLISHED BY

THE STANDARD PUBLISHING CO.,

CINCINNATI, O.

PREFACE

The studies composing this book were originally given before the members of the Northside Union Teacher-training Class in Cincinnati, O., 122 of whom passed a successful examination and received diplomas from the Ohio Sunday-school Association. If this book has any value, it will largely be because these lessons were tested before being printed.

As to the material in this book, we claim nothing original. Lessons of this character must present only the generally accepted facts and principles concerning the Bible and Bible-school work. As to the arrangement of material, a few definite outlines have been followed:

1. The Old Testament history is woven around sixteen leading characters. These characters are arranged in chronological order and are to be memorized.

2. The life of Christ is arranged in seven periods, with five important events in each period.

3. The general outline of the life of Paul is remembered by means of six periods and their subdivisions.

4. Bible geography is woven around three rivers, five mountains and twelve cities. Of the cities, three begin with B, three with C, three with J, and three with T. All geographical points, whether in Old or New Testament history, may be located by means of these rivers, mountains and cities.

5. Wherever possible, we have used "apt alliteration's artful aid." An example of this is found in Lesson XXXIX., where the five methods of securing attention all begin with C—Contact, Curiosity,* Concreteness, Co-operation, Contagion.

6. To direct study and make it definite, we have given the gist of the book in 289 "Drill Questions." These are found in the latter part of the book.

7. Our leading Sunday-school workers are rightly urging the introduction of supplemental work in all schools. This being true, a teacher-training course should cover the material that ought to be used as graded supplemental work. It is expected that those who complete this course will not only understand what supplemental work is, but be able to use it immediately in their teaching.

In working with Bible teachers of all religious bodies, I find an almost universal need of some plans that will enable the teacher to get and hold the general sweep of Bible history. In answer to this and other needs, this training course has been prepared.

As this book goes forth, it is with the hope that it may have a helpful ministry, and that those who study its contents may be led into a larger, happier and richer life in the service of our master Teacher.

2

REVISED EDITION.

In this revised edition of TRAINING FOR SERVICE, we give the original lessons carefully corrected, and eight additional lessons on the PUPIL. These additional lessons not only cover "child study," but those scholars who have outgrown childhood have as well been considered.

INTERNATIONAL APPROVAL.

This book has been approved by the Educational Committee of the International Sunday-school Association as meeting the requirements of the *First Standard Teacher-training Course*, and will be recognized accordingly by the various State and Provincial Associations.　　　　　　　　　　　　　　　　　　　　　　　　　　H. M.

LIST OF MAPS AND CHARTS.

CONTENTS

4

A FEW SUGGESTIONS

Training for Service

The Bible school is the richest, ripest and most responsive field of service within the church to-day. Those who labor in this field should be trained for their service. To answer this need, every church should have one or more training-classes.

Those Who Should Enter These Classes

Three classes of people ought to be in these classes: (1) All teachers and officers that are now at work in the Bible school; (2) all young people from sixteen years of age and older; (3) all parents who desire to know more about the Bible that they may better instruct their children.

The Requirements Met

At a joint meeting of the Educational Committee of the International Sunday-school Association and the leaders in teacher-training of the various religious bodies of America, which was held in Philadelphia, Pa., Jan. 7 and 8, 1908, a minimum amount of lessons was agreed upon for the FIRST STANDARD TEACHER-TRAINING COURSE. This course is to consist of fifty lessons as follows: Twenty on the Bible, seven on the pupil, seven on the principles of teaching, and seven on the Sunday-school. The other nine lessons necessary to complete the fifty may be upon these or other vital subjects according to the plan of the author. "TRAINING FOR SERVICE" (Revised) meets these requirements, and will be so recognized by the State and Provincial Sunday-school Associations. These fifty lessons may be taken in as many weeks, or a longer time may be consumed, according to the desire of the teacher and the class.

Getting Members for a Class

Announce it at every service of the church for a month or more before it begins. Start in for a large class. You ought to have twice as many in your class as you have teachers in your school. This will give you a reserve force, and make it possible to have in your teaching corps only those who are trained. Look forward to the time when you can place this motto in your Sunday-school room: "EVERY TEACHER IN THIS SCHOOL HAS A TEACHER-TRAINING DIPLOMA." Use your church membership, even if they are not in the school, as a source on which to draw for this class.

6

The Teacher

Get the very best person possible for the teacher. Perhaps your minister will take the first class. If you work up a large class for him, you will likely find that he will be delighted to take it. If you have no minister, you may be able to get a consecrated public-school teacher. At any rate, get some one, and start a class.

Drill Work

During this course the scholar is to learn a few foundation facts upon which he will ever afterwards build. This being true, these foundation facts must be well learned. Remember the old saying, "Not that which I can remember, but that which I can not forget, constitutes knowledge." Drill! Drill!! Drill!!! Review! Review!! Review!!! After you have gone over the lesson thoroughly and have answered from memory the "Test Questions" found at the close of each lesson, turn to the "Drill Questions" in the back of the book and drill on them till you never can forget them.

Individual Scholars

If you are in a community where there is no class, and you find it impossible to organize one, you can take this course alone. Scores of Christian workers are taking this course alone and are receiving their diplomas. Those who desire information concerning how the examination is given and the diplomas conferred in the case of individual students, may address the author of this book, Box 764, Cincinnati, O.

Graduation Exercises

A public recognition should be made of those who complete the course. This will not only serve to make the graduates feel more keenly their responsibility as Bible teachers, but it will create a desire in the hearts of some who attend the graduating exercises to take the course. Get the best speaker possible. Bring in somebody from outside. If your exercises are held during the week, you might charge a small admission fee. When the Northside Union Teacher-training Class graduated, March 26, 1907, eight thousand tickets were sold at ten and twenty cents. About $500 was spent for speakers, hall rent, flags, music, advertising and programs, and the committee had more than $400 over. What was the result? A few months after that graduation exercise so many wanted to take the course that five larger union teacher-training classes were formed in Greater Cincinnati. If you begin in time, and use the proper methods, you can fill the largest hall in your community when your class graduates.

The Diplomas

The diplomas are granted by the International Sunday-school Association through the various auxiliary associations. All classes and students should therefore enroll with their State or Provincial Association at the very beginning of their work. If you do not know to whom to write, address the "Teacher-training Department" of the International Sunday-school Association, Room 806, Hartford Bldg., Chicago, Ill.

Kinds of Classes

These lessons in Training for Service may be taken in classes organized in connection with the Bible school, or with the young people's societies, or with the mid-week prayer-meetings, and they may be used in advanced classes in place of the regular lesson. They may be begun at any time. Begin now and stick to it until you finish.

Some Reference Books

Every teacher should have a Bible dictionary, a concordance of the Bible, a book on Bible geography, and one or more books on Bible history, institutions and evidences. As there are so many covering these fields, we need not suggest any in particular. At this place, however, we desire to mention a few on pedagogy, psychology and general Sunday-school work:

Pedagogy

Primer on Teaching, by John Adams.
Bible School Pedagogy, by A. H. McKinney.
Seven Laws of Teaching, by John M. Gregory.
Teaching and Teachers, by H. Clay Trumbull.
Talks with the Training Class, by Margaret Slattery.
Teacher Training with the Master Teacher, by C. S. Beardsley.
Pedagogical Bible School, by Samuel B. Haslett.

Psychology

Psychology in Education, by Ruric N. Roark.
Talks to Teachers on Psychology, by Wm. James.
A Study of Child Nature, by Elizabeth Harrison.

General Sunday-school Work

Yale Lectures on the Sunday School, by H. Clay Trumbull.
How to Conduct a Sunday School, by Marion Lawrance.
The Front Line of Sunday School Work, by A. N. Peloubet.

PART I.

THREE LESSONS ON THE BIBLE AND ITS BOOKS

LESSON   I.   THE BIBLE AND ITS DIVISIONS.
LESSON II.   THE BOOKS OF THE OLD TESTAMENT.
LESSON III.   THE BOOKS OF THE NEW TESTAMENT.

LESSON I. THE BIBLE AND ITS DIVISIONS

I. The word "Bible" comes from the Greek word **biblos**, which means "book." There is only one book in the world that is worthy of being called the Book.

II. Two names of the Bible found in the Book itself are: (1) Word of God (Eph. 6: 17); (2) Scriptures (Matt. 21: 42; John 5: 39; Acts 17: 11; 2 Tim. 3: 15).

III. The Bible is divided into two parts, familiarly known as the Old Testament and the New Testament. Paul tells of the old

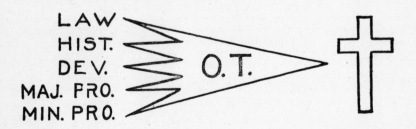

covenant (2 Cor. 3: 14, R. V.) and the new covenant (2 Cor. 3: 6, R. V.). The Latin rendering of the Greek word **diatheka** (covenant) is **testamentum**—testament.

IV. There are thirty-nine books in the Old Testament.

Memory Help: O-l-d, 3; T-e-s-t-a-m-e-n-t, 9; suggesting 39.

V. There are twenty-seven books in the New Testament.

Memory Help: N-e-w, 3; T-e-s-t-a-m-e-n-t, 9; 3 x 9 equals 27.

VI. The books of the Old Testament are divided into five parts: **Law, History, Devotion, Major Prophets, Minor Prophets.**

VII. Of the books of **Law,** there are five; of **History,** twelve; of **Devotion,** five; of **Major Prophets,** five; of **Minor Prophets,** twelve.

VIII. The books of the New Testament are divided into five parts: **Biography, History, Special Letters, General Letters, Prophecy.**

IX. Of the books of **Biography** there are four; of **History,** one; of **Special Letters,** fourteen; of **General Letters,** seven; of **Prophecy,** one.

BLACKBOARD WORK.

| THE BIBLE | 1. Meaning of word.
2. Two names.
3. Its divisions. | O. T. | 1. Law. 5
2. Hist. 12
3. Dev. 5
4. Maj. Pro. 5
5. Mi. Pro. 12
— 39 | N. T. | 1. Biog. 4
2. Hist. 1
3. Sp. Let. 14
4. Ge. Let. 7
5. Proph. 1
— 27 |

TEST QUESTIONS.

1. What does the word "Bible" mean?
2. Give two names of the Bible found in the Book itself.
3. What are the divisions of the books of the Bible?
4. How many books in the Old Testament? Give the memory help.
5. How many books in the New Testament? Give the memory help.
6. How many books in the whole Bible?
7. Give the divisions of the books of the Old Testament, and the **number of** books in each.
8. Give the divisions of the books of the New Testament, and the **number of** books in each.

LESSON II. THE BOOKS OF THE OLD TESTAMENT

Every Christian should be thoroughly familiar with the names and order of the books of the Bible. Without such familiarity, it will be impossible to use the Bible as we should. In our last lesson, we learned the divisions of the Old Testament. These were **Law, History, Devotion, Major Prophets, Minor Prophets.** We will now learn the names of the books in each one of these divisions.

I. The books of the **Law** (also called **Pentateuch**) are five: Genesis, Exodus, Leviticus, Numbers, Deuteronomy.

II. The books of **History** are twelve: Joshua, Judges, Ruth, 1 Samuel, 2 Samuel, 1 Kings, 2 Kings, 1 Chronicles, 2 Chronicles, Ezra, Nehemiah, Esther.

III. The books of **Devotion** are five: Job, Psalms, Proverbs, Ecclesiastes, Song of Solomon.

IV. The books of the **Major Prophets** are five: Isaiah, Jeremiah, Lamentations, Ezekiel, Daniel.

V. The books of the **Minor Prophets** are twelve: Hosea, Joel,

Amos, Obadiah, Jonah, Micah, Nahum, Habakkuk, Zephaniah, Haggai, Zechariah, Malachi.

NOTE.—There have been various plans for remembering the books of the Minor Prophets, most of which are as hard to remember as the books themselves. The best way for the student to do is to go over and over them until they can be said with absolute ease.

BLACKBOARD WORK.

LAW	G., E., L., N., D.	HIST.	J., J., R., 1 S., 2 S., 1 K., 2 K., 1 C., 2 C., E., N., E.			
DEVOTION	J., P., P., E., S. of S.	MAJ. P.	I., J., L., E., D.	MIN. P.	H., J., A., O., J., M., N., H., Z., H., Z., M.	

TEST QUESTIONS.

1. Name the divisions of the books of the Old Testament.
2. Name the books of Law.
3. Name the books of History.
4. Name the books of Devotion.
5. Name the books of the Major Prophets.
6. Name the books of the Minor Prophets.
7. How long does it take you to repeat the books of the Old Testament?

LESSON III. THE BOOKS OF THE NEW TESTAMENT

I. The Divisions of the Books of the New Testament.

1. **Biography.** Four books.
2. **History.** One book.
3. **Special Letters.** Fourteen books.
4. **General Letters.** Seven books.
5. **Prophecy.** One book.

II. The Names of the Books of the New Testament.

1. The books of **Biography** are Matthew, Mark, Luke, John. These are called the **Gospels.** The first three are called the "synoptic" Gospels. **Synoptic** comes from the Greek word which means to "view together." As these Gospels are in many ways similar, we say the writers "view together" the life of Christ.

2. The one book of **History** is Acts.

3. The **Special Letters** are Romans, 1 Corinthians, 2 Corinthians, Galatians, Ephesians, Philippians, Colossians, 1 Thessalonians, 2 Thessalonians, 1 Timothy, 2 Timothy, Titus, Philemon, Hebrews.

4. The **General Letters** are James, 1 Peter, 2 Peter, 1 John, 2 John, 3 John, Jude.

NOTE.—Second and Third John are classed under the "General" Letters, although they were written to individual Christians.

5. The one book of **Prophecy** is Revelation.

III. Writers of the Books of the New Testament.

1. The books of **Biography** were written by those whose names they bear. Matthew and John were apostles.

2. **Acts** was written by Luke.

3. The **Special Letters** (except Hebrews) were written by Paul. Concerning Hebrews the authorship is uncertain. It is placed among the Pauline letters because it is Pauline in teaching.

4. The **General Letters** were written by those whose names they bear.

5. **Revelation** was written by John. Thus we see that of the books of the New Testament, Luke wrote two; John, five, and Paul, thirteen. If Paul wrote the Hebrew letter, he wrote fourteen.

LAW / HIST. / DEV. / MAJ. PRO. / MIN. PRO. — O.T. + N.T. — BIOG. / HIST. / SP. LE. / GE. LE. / PRO.

BLACKBOARD WORK.

Biography : M., M., L., J.
History : A.
Spe. Letters : R., 1 C., 2 C., G., E., P., C., 1 T., 2 T., 1 T., 2 T., T., P., H.
Gen Letters : J., 1 P., 2 P., 1 J., 2 J., 3 J., J.
Prophecy : R.

TEST QUESTIONS.

1. Name the divisions of the books of the New Testament.
2. Name the books of Biography.
3. Name the book of History.
4. Name the General Letters.
5. Name the Special Letters.
6. Name the book of Prophecy.
7. Name the "synoptic" Gospels.
8. Name the books of the New Testament written by the following men: Matthew, Mark, Luke, John, Peter, Paul, James, Jude.
9. Name the two Gospels written by apostles.

PART II.

TWO LESSONS ON EVIDENCES

LESSON IV. EIGHT REASONS WHY I BELIEVE THE BIBLE IS THE WORD OF GOD.
LESSON V. EIGHT REASONS WHY I BELIEVE THAT JESUS IS THE CHRIST, THE SON OF GOD.

LESSON IV. EIGHT REASONS WHY I BELIEVE THE BIBLE IS THE WORD OF GOD

In Heb. 1: 1, 2 we read one of the many claims the Bible makes to being the revealed word of God. The book is full of "Thus saith the Lord" and "Verily, I say unto you." There are a great many reasons for believing these claims of divine origin. The following have been sufficient to satisfy many minds:

I. **Because it meets the needs of human life.** Under all circumstances man can go to the Bible and find help. The Bible fits perfectly into human experiences.

II. **Because of its wonderful unity.**

This book was written by some forty men widely separated by time, culture, training and language. In spite of the lapse of time and composite authorship, the book as a whole makes an impression of unity upon the mind of the student. So strong is the sense of unity that we would feel a distinct loss if any one of the books should suddenly be lost from the collection.

III. **Because it is superior to all other books.**

There is no book that is so widely or repeatedly read. Among books it is immortal; few books outlive their authors. It is the oldest book in the world, but is still of vital interest to each generation, which fact shows that it treats on subjects of eternal freshness.

When the Revised Version came out, a great daily paper published the whole New Testament in its regular edition. Within forty-eight hours after its publication two million and a half copies were sold. The Bible must be classed with the indestructible things.

IV. **Because of its influence upon the world.**

"By their fruits ye shall know them," is the safest foundation for judgment ever laid down. If you draw a line around the countries where the greatest freedom is enjoyed and the highest civili-

13

zation flourishes, you will find that you have included the countries where the people believe in Christianity, and excluded those where it has very little or no influence. Wherever the Bible has gone it has sweetened the home, exalted womanhood, sanctified the cradle and redeemed men.

V. Because of the character of those who accept it.

Business propositions are often turned down, merely because of the class of men who are promoting them. Who are the men in your community who believe the Bible and are endeavoring to live by it? Who are the men who are opposed to the Bible? Is it hard to decide which class is the better and doing the more for the world and men?

VI. Because it reveals the way of salvation.

It is the answer to the soul's greatest question, "What must I do to be saved?" It treats of the grandest subjects in a way that brings peace and satisfaction to the most powerful as well as humble minds. No book can treat of more exalted themes than God, Christ, sin, man, salvation, righteousness. These are the themes on which the book discourses.

VII. Because man unaided could not have produced the Bible.

Well has Alfred M. Haggard said, "I know that no man made the roses. I know that no man painted the sunset on the evening skies. In the same way I know that no man, nor set of men, unaided, have produced the Bible. It points to God as certainly as the flowers or the heavens."

VIII. Because those who grow in holiness cherish the Bible more and more.

In our growth we outgrow most things that at one time aided us. We outgrow our schools and many of our books, and sometimes our companions; but nobody has ever outgrown the Bible. Some have grown away from it, but none have outgrown it. The greatest saints have been the most ardent believers and students of the Book. As they have grown in holiness they have grown in their love for the Book. If it were the product of man, surely some one would have outgrown or graduated from the Book long since. Is there another book in the world that some men have not outgrown?

BLACKBOARD WORK.

REASONS FOR BELIEVING THE BIBLE TO BE GOD'S WORD.

1. Meets the needs—.	5. Character of—.
2. Wonderful unity.	6. Reveals the way—.
3. Superior to all—.	7. Man unaided could—.
4. Influence upon—.	8. Grow in holiness—.

Acknowledgment: Mr. Claude Percy Leach rendered valuable assistance in the preparation of this lesson.

TEST QUESTION.

1. Give five reasons why you believe the Bible is the word of God.

LESSON V. EIGHT REASONS WHY I BELIEVE THAT JESUS IS THE CHRIST, THE SON OF GOD

To the Christian, Christ is all and in all. His name rises above every human name. His life is the model life. His worth overshadows the world's wealth. His light dispels darkness, and is above that of the brightness of the sun. The Christian life is the transcendent life.

There is no condemnation for them who are in Christ Jesus: yea, even death, for the Christian, is an entrance into a better life.

"I am the resurrection and the life: he that believeth on me, though he die, yet shall he live: and whosoever liveth and believeth on me shall never die."—Jesus.

I BELIEVE THAT JESUS CHRIST IS THE SON OF GOD:

I. **Because I believe in the Bible, and the Bible declares Him to be the Son of God.** To take Christ out of the Bible is like taking the sun from the solar system. Matt. 1: 21; Mark 1: 1; 3: 11; Acts 13: 33; Ps. 2: 7; Isa. 53: 3; John 3: 31; Matt. 8: 29; 3: 17; Tit. 2: 13; Luke 1: 35; Acts 5: 31.

II. **Because Jesus fulfilled prophecy, and thus is the Messiah of the Old Testament, the anointed Saviour, the Son of God.** Notice the following passages in pairs: Isa. 7: 14; Matt. 1: 22, 23; Hos. 11: 1; Matt. 2: 15; Jer. 31: 15; Matt. 2: 16-18; Isa. 40: 3; Matt. 3: 3; Isa. 53: 4-6, 12; Matt. 20: 28; Mic. 5: 2; Luke 2: 27, 28; Zech. 13: 7; Matt. 26: 56; Isa. 53: 7; Matt. 26: 63; 27: 12; Isa. 52: 14; 53: 3; John 19: 5; Ps. 22: 16; John 19: 18; 20: 25; Ps. 22: 18; Matt. 27: 35; Isa. 53: 12; Mark 15: 28; Isa. 53:9; Matt. 27: 57-60; Ps. 16: 10; Acts 2: 31.

III. **Because Jesus was superior to every human being.** Notice the great "I AM'S:"

"I AM the good Shepherd," John 10: 11.
"I AM the Way," John 14: 6.
"I AM the Truth," John 14: 6.
"I AM the Life," John 14: 6.
"I AM the true Vine," John 15: 1.
"I AM the bright morning star," Rev. 22: 16.
"I AM the bread of life," John 6: 35.
"I AM Jesus," Acts. 26: 15; Matt. 1: 21.
"I AM the Resurrection," John 11: 25.

IV. **Because no one was able to convict Him of sin.** John 8: 46. He was in all points tempted like as we are, yet without sin. Heb. 4: 15; Mark 1: 24; John 8: 46; 1 Pet. 1: 19; 2: 22; 1 John 3: 5.

V. **Because of the impression He made on his contemporaries.** John 7: 46; John 3: 2; Matt. 7: 29; Mark 1: 22.

VI. **Because the enemies of Christ declare his claims to be true.** Pilate says: "I find no fault in this man" (Luke 23: 4; John 18: 38). Pilate's wife says: "Have thou nothing to do with that righteous man" (Matt. 27: 19). Judas says: "I have sinned in that I have betrayed innocent blood" (Matt. 27: 4). The unclean spirit says: "I know thee, who thou art, the holy One of God" (Mark 1: 24).

VII. **Because there is no other way to explain the effect of His life and teachings upon the world.** To say that an empty story has for twenty centuries inspired the greatest thoughts, transformed and moulded the highest lives, would be the folly of follies. All human history moves around Christ as its center.

VIII. **Because He is the risen Saviour.** This is the pivotal fact of Christianity. Around this truth all other truths of God revolve. (Matt. 28: 6; 1 Cor. 15: 20.)

BLACKBOARD WORK.

REASONS FOR BELIEVING THAT JESUS IS THE CHRIST, THE SON OF GOD.

1. Bible declares Him—.
2. Fulfilled prophecy.
3. Superior to every—.
4. No one was able—.
5. Impression He—.
6. Enemies declare—.
7. No other way to—.
8. Risen Saviour.

TEST QUESTION.

1. Give five reasons for believing that Jesus is the Christ, the Son of God.

PART III.

SIX LESSONS ON OLD TESTAMENT HISTORY

LESSON VI. OLD TESTAMENT HISTORY BY CHARACTERS

All persons, I am sure, have felt the need of some plan for remembering the order of events of Old Testament history. When we want to be sure of the number of days in the month we go over the old rhyme,

"Thirty days have September," etc.

In this lesson we want to give a somewhat similar plan for answering the many questions that will confront us concerning the events of Old Testament history. We are going to ask you to learn sixteen characters in Old Testament history, in the order as they lived. This will be, so to speak, the alphabet of Old Testament history. The history of the sixteen leading characters and their associates will connect the entire story from the creation to the close of the Old Testament records. These sixteen are Adam, Noah, Abraham, Joseph, Moses, Joshua, Gideon, Samuel, Saul, David, Solomon, Elijah, Isaiah, Jeremiah, Daniel and Nehemiah. The story of Old Testament history may be recalled by means of these sixteen names.

I. **Adam.**—With Adam are connected all things pertaining to the beginning of the world—man, sin and redemption. With him we associate Eve, Cain and Abel. Eve was the first woman, Cain the first murderer, Abel the first martyr.

II. **Noah.**—The first sin was not the only one, and the sacred record tells us that man became so sinful that it was necessary for God to destroy all save those who would serve him. Every-

17

thing pertaining to the calling of the world to repentance just previous to the flood, the building of the ark, the flood, the repeopling
of the world after the flood, are associated with Noah. The persons associated with him are his three sons, Shem, Ham and
Japheth.

III. **Abraham.**—After the world was repeopled subsequent to the
flood, the inhabitants were scattered throughout the world. This
dispersion took place from Babel (Gen. 11: 1-9). The next great
character in history after Noah, is Abraham. God wanted to call
a nation through whom he might speak his will more perfectly to
the world. Abraham was called to be head of this nation. With
him we associate Lot, Isaac and Jacob. Lot was Abraham's
nephew. Isaac was Abraham's son, whom he was commanded to
offer up as a sacrifice. Jacob was Isaac's son, and the father of the
twelve well-known sons of Israel.

IV. **Joseph.**—Everything pertaining to the sojourn and oppression of the Israelites in Egypt is associated with Joseph, one of the
twelve sons of Jacob. The persons associated with him are Reuben,
Pharaoh and Benjamin. Reuben was his oldest brother; Pharaoh,
the ruler of Egypt (the Pharaoh intended here is the Pharaoh of
the oppression, known as Rameses II.); Benjamin, the youngest
brother of Joseph.

V. **Moses.**—It was during the oppression in Egypt that Moses
was born. It was Joseph who made it possible for the Israelites to
be in Egypt, and it was Moses who led them out of Egypt under the
oppression of Pharaoh. With him are associated Jethro, Aaron
and Nadab. Jethro was Moses' father-in-law; Aaron was his brother; Nadab was Aaron's son, who was killed because he offered
strange fire before the Lord.

ADAM, SETH, ENOS, CAINAN, MAHALALEEL, JARED, ENOCH, METHUSALEH,
LAMECH, NOAH, SHEM, ARPHAXAD, SALAH, EBER, PELEG, REU, SERUG,
NAHOR, TERAH, ABRAHAM.

It is comparatively easy to follow from generation to generation, from Abraham to
the end of Old Testament history. The above outline will show where Abraham
belongs.

VI. **Joshua.**—Moses died on the eve of leading the Israelites
into the land of Canaan. Joshua immediately took up this work,
led the Israelites across the Jordan, conquered Jericho, and helped
them settle in the land of Canaan. With him are associated Caleb,
Achan and Eleazar. Caleb was one of the twelve spies whom Moses
sent into Canaan. The Bible says that he "wholly followed the
Lord;" Achan was the man who stole the wedge of gold; Eleazar
was Aaron's son, and his successor as high priest.

VII. **Gideon.**—After Joshua's death we have what is called the
"reign of the judges." Of these there were fifteen. Gideon was
one of the greatest. With Gideon we associate Samson, Deborah
and Ruth. Samson was a man of wonderful physical strength;
Deborah was the woman judge (all the other judges being men);
Ruth was a daughter-in-law of Naomi, and an ancestress of Christ.

VIII. **Samuel.**—The last one of the fifteen judges was Samuel. With him we associate Hannah, Eli and Joel. Hannah was Samuel's mother; Eli was a high priest and next to the last judge; Joel was Samuel's oldest son.

BLACKBOARD WORK.

NOTE.—The most important thing in the preparation of this lesson is to learn to repeat with absolute ease the characters given in the blackboard below. This may not seem essential now, but it will be found of vital importance later. The whole class should repeat these eight in concert.

Eight Persons: A. N. A. J. M. J. G. S.

TEST QUESTIONS.

1. Name eight leading characters in Old Testament history in order, beginning with Adam and ending with Samuel.
2. What three persons do you associate with Adam?
3. What great event do you associate with Noah?
4. What happened at Babel?
5. Into what country was Joseph taken when he was sold by his brothers?
6. Who was Joseph's father? His youngest brother? His oldest brother?
7. In what country was Moses born?
8. Who was Jethro? Aaron?
9. Who was Moses' successor? What great thing did he do?
10. What reign follows Joshua's death?
11. How many "judges" were there?
12. Who was the last one of the "judges"?

LESSON VII. OLD TESTAMENT HISTORY BY CHARACTERS (Concluded)

In this lesson we are given the latter half of the sixteen characters of Old Testament history and their associates. Commit these sixteen characters so you can easily repeat them. The three associate characters need not be committed at present. The student should, however, be so familiar with them that he could associate any one of them, when necessary, with the proper ones of the sixteen characters. For instance, if Lot is named, the student should immediately associate him with Abraham. Or, if Achan is mentioned, he should be associated with Joshua.

I. **Saul.**—Samuel, who was the last one of the eight characters mentioned in our last lesson, anointed Saul as the first king of the Jewish nation. With Saul we associate Kish, Jonathan and Abner. Kish was Saul's father; Jonathan was his oldest son and David's friend; Abner was a cousin of Saul and his great general.

II. **David.**—The second king of the Jewish nation was David. With him we associate Goliath, Nathan and Absalom. Goliath was the giant whom David killed; Nathan was a prophet who rebuked David; Absalom was David's wicked son.

III. **Solomon.**—The third king of the Jews was Solomon. With him we associate the Queen of Sheba, Rehoboam and Jeroboam. The Queen of Sheba was the queen who came a long way to ask Solomon hard questions (1 Kings 10: 1); Rehoboam was Solomon's son, and the first king of Judah; Jeroboam was the first king of the divided kingdom of Israel. The kingdom of Judah occupied the southern part, and the kingdom of Israel the northern part, of Canaan.

IV. Elijah.—After Solomon's death there are no more great kings of the united kingdom of the Jews, so we associate history from this time on around prophets. The first great one we mention is Elijah, who lived at the time of King Ahab. With Elijah we associate Ahab, Elisha and Naaman. Ahab was the seventh king of Israel and the husband of Jezebel; Elisha was Elijah's successor, and Naaman was the leper who came to Elisha to be healed.

V. Isaiah.—Following Elijah, we have the great gospel prophet, Isaiah. It was he who prophesied when Israel was taken captive. With Isaiah we associate Hezekiah, Manasseh and Sennacherib. Hezekiah was the king of Judah when Israel was taken captive; Manasseh was the son of Hezekiah, who began to reign over Judah when but twelve years of age, and reigned for fifty-five years; Sennacherib was the king of Assyria whose great army was slain by an "angel of the Lord."

VI. Jeremiah.—When we think of Isaiah, we naturally think of another great prophet—his name was Jeremiah. He is called the weeping prophet. With Jeremiah we associate Huldah, Jehoiakim and Zedekiah. Huldah was the prophetess who told Josiah of the captivity of Judah; Jehoiakim was the king of Judah who burned the word of God; Zedekiah was the twentieth and last king of Judah.

VII. Daniel.—Before Jeremiah's death the great man of the Babylonian captivity enters into Bible history. His name was Daniel. With him we associate Nebuchadnezzar, Belshazzar and Cyrus. Nebuchadnezzar was the king of Babylon when Daniel was carried there a captive; Belshazzar was the wicked king to whom God spoke through the handwriting on the wall; Cyrus was the king of Persia who permitted the Jews to return to Jerusalem.

VIII. Nehemiah.—After the Jews returned to Jerusalem at the permission of Cyrus, many important events occurred that are associated with the name of Nehemiah. He was the governor of Judea who directed the rebuilding of the walls of Jerusalem. With Nehemiah we associate Zechariah, Ezra and Malachi. Zechariah was the man who had eight visions; Ezra was a priest and a leader of the people; Malachi was the last one of the Minor Prophets.

BLACKBOARD WORK.

16: A. N. A. J. M. J. G. S. S. D. S. E. I. J. D. N.

TEST QUESTIONS.

1. Name in order sixteen leading characters in Old Testament history.
2. Who was Saul's father? His oldest son?
3. Who was the first king of the Jews?
4. Who was the second king of the Jews?
5. Who was the third king of the Jews?
6. When the kingdom of the Jews was divided, what was the northern part called? The southern part?
7. Who was the first king of Judah?
8. Who was the first king of Israel?
9. What great prophet lived at the time of King Ahab?
10. Who was Elijah's successor?
11. Who was the "gospel" prophet? The "weeping" prophet?
12. What great man of the Babylonian captivity interpreted the "handwriting on the wall"?
13. What governor of Judea directed the rebuilding of the walls of Jerusalem?
14. Who was Ezra? Malachi?

LESSON VIII. OLD TESTAMENT HISTORY BY PERIODS

THE FIRST TWO PERIODS

1. The Old Testament can be best understood by seeing the entire history in its development.

2. Old Testament history may be divided into six periods.*

I. **Probation.**

II. **Preparation.**

III. **Conquest.**

IV. **Power.**

V. **Decline.**

VI. **Servitude.**

I. **Probation.**—The period of **Probation** begins with **Adam** and ends with **Noah.** The dates during this period are uncertain. Usher puts the creation B. C. 4004, but it is now thought by many scholars that the time between Adam and Christ was much longer than four thousand years. The first eleven chapters of Genesis cover this period.

1. **Events.**—In this period we call attention to three important events:

(1) The **Fall,** which brought sin into the world (Gen. 3: 6).

(2) The **Promise of Redemption,** which brought hope into the world (Gen. 3: 15).

(3) The **Deluge** (Gen. 7: 11, 12). Only those who obeyed God were saved.

2. **Persons.**—In this period we call attention to two important Persons:

(1) **Adam,** with whom we associate the **Fall** and the **Promise of Redemption.**

(2) **Noah,** with whom we associate the **Deluge.**

NOTE.—These are two of the sixteen leading characters given in Lessons VI. and VII. Write all of them out and learn them until you can repeat them with absolute ease. Associate every event and person in Old Testament history with one of them.

---

*The periods are suggested by Dr. H. M. Hamill in his "Normal Bible and Training Lessons."

II. Preparation.—The period of **Preparation** extends from **Noah** to the call of **Moses;** *i. e.*, from the **Deluge** to the **Exodus.** During this period Abraham was called to be the head of a chosen nation. Abraham and his descendants were chosen, not because God loved them more than others, but because through them he was to bless the world.

    1. **Events.**—In this period attention is called to three events:

        (1) **The Dispersion** (Gen. 11: 9). This was at Babel in Chaldea.

        (2) **Journeys of the Patriarchs** (Gen. 12, 13, 20, etc.). This covers the journeys of Abraham, Isaac and Jacob.

        (3) **Experiences in Egypt** (Gen. 46-50, etc.). Some time in the life of Jacob, he and his family went down into Egypt, where they sojourned for over four hundred years. Toward the close of the sojourn the Israelites endured a cruel bondage, which was broken by the Exodus under the leadership of Moses.

    2. **Persons.**—In this period are several important **persons,** two of whom we mention:

        (1) **Abraham,** the man who was called to leave home (Gen. 12: 1).

        (2) **Joseph,** the greatest of the twelve sons of Jacob.

BLACKBOARD WORK.

Persons:	A. N.	A. J. M. J. G. S.		S. D. S.	E. I. J.	D. N.
Periods:	Pro.	Prep.				
Events:	F. P. R. D.	D. J. P. E. E.				

TEST QUESTIONS.

1. Name in order sixteeen leading characters in Old Testament history.
2. Name the six periods of Old Testament history.
3. What is the extent of the period of Probation?
4. Name three events in this period.
5. Name two persons in this period.
6. Give the extent of the period of Preparation.
7. Name three events in this period.
8. Name two persons in this period.
9. Connect one event with each of the following: Adam, Noah, Abraham, Joseph.

LESSON IX. OLD TESTAMENT HISTORY BY PERIODS (Continued)

THE SECOND AND THIRD PERIODS

III. Conquest.—The period of **Conquest** began with the **call of Moses** and ended with the **coronation of Saul.** During this period the Israelites left Egypt, traveled through the wilderness, conquered Canaan, and passed through the trying years of the rule of the judges.

It should be noted here that the **birth** of Moses comes in the

period of **Preparation,** while all of his work after his call comes in
the period of **Conquest.**

1. **Events.**—Three important events in the period of **Conquest**
are:

> (1) **Experiences in the Wilderness (Ex. 13 ff.).*** Moses
> led the Israelites out of Egypt, across the Red Sea, and
> through the wilderness. He died on Mt. Nebo, when the
> Israelites were ready to enter Canaan.
>
> (2) **Conquest of Canaan (Josh. 3 ff.).** After the death of
> Moses, Joshua led the Israelites in the conquest of Jeri-
> cho and Canaan, and helped them to settle in that land.
>
> (3) **Rule of the Judges.**—There were fifteen judges, of
> whom Deborah, Gideon, Samson and Samuel were the
> greatest.

2. **Persons.**—There were many heroes during this period. We
mention four here:

> (1) **Moses,** the man who led the Israelites out of Egypt
> (Ex. 3: 10).
>
> (2) **Joshua,** Moses' successor, and the man who led the
> Israelites into Canaan (Josh. 3 ff.).
>
> (3) **Gideon,** one of the greatest of the fifteen judges (Judg.
> 7 ff.).
>
> (4) **Samuel,** the last judge. Samuel anointed both Saul
> and David as kings (1 Sam. 10: 1; 16: 13).

IV. **Power.**—The period of **Power** begins with the **coronation
of Saul** and ends with the **death of Solomon.** This covers the history of the United Kingdom. Saul's coronation was probably B. C.
1037, and Solomon's death, 937 (or B. C. 1095 and B. C. 975
respectively, according to Usher).

1. **Events.**—Three important events during this period are:

> (1) **Saul's Defeat.** Saul was defeated by the Philistines
> and met his death at Gilboa (1 Sam. 31: 1-13).
>
> (2) **Ark Removed.** David captured Jerusalem from the
> Jebusites and removed thither the ark (2 Sam. 6).
>
> (3) **Temple Built.** During Solomon's reign, a magnificent
> temple was built on Mt. Moriah (1 Kings 6 ff.). More
> will be said about this temple in a later chapter.

2. **Persons.**—The three greatest men of this period are:

> (1) **Saul,** the first king of the United Kingdom.
>
> (2) **David,** the second king of the United Kingdom.
>
> (3) **Solomon,** the third and last king of the United Kingdom.

BLACKBOARD WORK.

Persons: Periods: Events:	A. N. Pro. { F. { P. R. { D.	A. J. M. Prep. { D. { J. P. { E. E	J. G. S. Con. { E. W. { C. C. { R. J.	S. D. S. Pow. { S. D. { A. R. { T. B.	E. I. J.	D. N.

---

* ff means "and following."

TEST QUESTIONS.

1. Name in order sixteen leading characters in **Old Testament history.**
2. Name the six periods of Old Testament history
3. What is the extent of the period of Conquest?
4. Name three events in this period.
5. Name four persons in this period.
6. Give the extent of the period of Power.
7. Name three events in this period.
8. Name three persons in this period.
9. Name the first three kings of the United Kingdom of the Jews.
10. Tell something about each of the following men: Moses, Joshua, Gideon, Samuel, Saul, David, Solomon.

LESSON X. OLD TESTAMENT HISTORY BY PERIODS (Concluded)

THE LAST TWO PERIODS.

V. Decline.—The period of **Decline** began at the death of Solomon and ended with the beginning of Daniel's active career; *i. e.*, from the **division** of the kingdom to the Babylonian **captivity.** When the kingdom was divided, Rehoboam, Solomon's son, became the king of Judah, and Jeroboam became the king of Israel. The kingdom of Israel was governed by nineteen kings, and ended with the fall of Samaria (B. C. 721), at which time the ten tribes were carried into captivity in Assyria and were lost (2 Kings 17). The kingdom of Judah remained a kingdom until it was captured by the Chaldeans (B. C. 587), and carried to Babylon (2 Chron. 36).

1. **Epochs.**—This period naturally divides itself into two epochs:*

(1) **Division.**—The epoch of division was from the division of the kingdom to the end of the kingdom of Israel (1 Kings 12 ff.; 2 Kings 17: 6).

(2) **Decay.**—The epoch of decay was from the end of the kingdom of Israel to the captivity of the kingdom of Judah (2 Kings 24).

2. **Persons.**—During this period we have all the kings of the kingdoms of Judah and Israel. As there were so many of these, most of them of minor importance, we look for others as centers around which we may entwine the history of this period. Hence we turn from kings to prophets and mention three of the greatest:

(1) **Elijah,** the great prophet who lived at the time of King Ahab (1 Kings 17: 1 ff.).

(2) **Isaiah,** the "gospel prophe ," who prophesied when the kingdom of Israel was taken captive.

(3) **Jeremiah,** the "weeping prophet," who prophesied when the kingdom of Judah was taken into Babylonian captivity (Jer. 21 ff.).

VI. Servitude.—The period of **Servitude** began with **Daniel, and** ended with **Christ.** It extended from the Babylonian captivity to the advent of our Saviour.

---

*The terms "Division" and "Decay" were suggested by J. L. Hurlbut in his "Revised Normal Outlines."

1. **Epochs.**—This period divides itself naturally into five epochs:
   (1) **Chaldean Rule.**—The Chaldean rule was a half century in duration. It began with the Babylonian captivity (B. C. 587), and ended with the conquest of Babylon by Cyrus, the great Persian ruler—B. C. 536 (2 Chron. 36: 20).
   (2) **Persian Rule.**—The Persian rule began with the conquest of Babylon by Cyrus (B. C. 536), and ended with the overthrow of the Persian Empire by Alexander the Great (B. C. 330). During this period the Jews were permitted to return to Jerusalem (Ez. 1: 1 ff.), where they were allowed to govern themselves under the general supervision of the Persian rulers.
   (3) **Greek Rule.**—Under Greek supremacy the Jews lived in Palestine more than one hundred and fifty years. During this period many of the Jews were induced to settle in Alexandria in Egypt, where a new Jewish center was formed. Through influences there, Jewish thought was somewhat modified by Grecian philosophy. A most important result of the Jewish settlement in Alexandria was the translation of the Old Testament into Greek, and circulating it in many places, thus preparing the way for Christianity.
   (4) **Maccabean Freedom.**—At the death of Alexander the Great, the kingdom was divided between rival generals. All went well as long as Jerusalem remained under the power of Egypt, but when Syria attained supremacy, the Jews were oppressed, and an attempt was made to blot out the true religion and substitute Grecian idolatries. This incited Judas Maccabeus to lead the Jews in a revolt. This was successful, and for a century and a quarter the people were ruled by a line of princes called Asmoneans, or Maccabeans, and enjoyed large political freedom.
   (5) **Roman Rule.**—The Jews were finally compelled to yield to the Romans. Herod the Great received the title of king from the Roman Senate in the year B. C. 40. From that time the Jewish provinces were considered a part of the Roman Empire, although the Jews were allowed to administer in religious matters. Herod, who was the king when Christ was born (Matt. 2: 1-18), was Herod the Great. Thus we see the connecting history between the Old and New Testaments.
2. **Persons.**—Five persons of this period, aside from those mentioned above, are:
   (1) **Daniel,** the man who dared to live right, away from home.
   (2) **Nehemiah,** the governor of Judea, who directed the rebuilding of the walls of Jerusalem.
   (3) **Zechariah,** the man who had eight visions.
   (4) **Ezra,** the scribe who was one of Nehemiah's efficient coworkers.
   (5) **Malachi,** the last one of the Minor Prophets.

BLACKBOARD WORK.

Persons:	A. N.	A. J. M. J. G. S.	S. D. S.	E. I. J.	D. N.
Periods:	Pro.	Prep. Con.	Pow.	Dec.	Serv.
Events:	F. P. R. D.	D. J. P. E. E.	E. W. C. C. R. J.	S. D. A. R. T. B.	D. D.	C. R. P. R. G. R. M. F. R. R.
Dates:		2348 1491 1037	937	587	

Outline Showing Sweep of History from Adam to Christ.

EIGHT DATES TO REMEMBER IN OLD TESTAMENT HISTORY.

The flood, B. C. 2348 (Usher).
The call of Abraham, B. C. 1921 (Usher).
The exodus from Egypt, B. C. 1491 (Usher).
Coronation of Saul, B. C. 1095 (Usher) or B. C. 1037.
Division of the kingdom, B. C. 975 (Usher) or B. C. 937.
Fall of Samaria, B. C. 721.
Babylonian captivity, B. C. 587.
Return from captivity, B. C. 536.

TEST QUESTIONS.

1. Name in order sixteen leading characters in Old Testament history.
2. Name the six periods of Old Testament history.
3. What is the extent of the period of Decline?
4. Name two epochs in this period.
5. Name three persons in this period.
6. What is the extent of the period of Servitude?
7. Name five epochs in this period.
8. Name five persons in this period.
9. Give the following dates: Flood; Call of Abraham; Exodus from Egypt; Coronation of Saul; Division of the Kingdom; Fall of Samaria; Babylonian Captivity; Return from Captivity.
10. Who was Cyrus? Alexander the Great? Judas Maccabeus? Herod the Great?
11. What relation was the Herod mentioned in Matt. 2:1 to Herod the Great?

LESSON XI. REVIEW OF OLD TESTAMENT HISTORY

In your review use the questions found in the back of the book and go over carefully the first eighty-nine questions. Study especially Questions 31 to 89, inclusive. If you can answer all of those drill questions, you will be sure to pass a successful examination.

CHART ON OLD TESTAMENT HISTORY
FROM ADAM TO CHRIST.

PERSONS .	Adam, Noah.	Abr. Jos. Mos. Jo. Gi. Sa.		Saul, David, Sol.	Elij. Isa. Jer.	Daniel, Nehemiah.
PERIODS . . .	PROBATION.	PREPARATION.	CONQUEST.	POWER.	DECLINE.	SERVITUDE.
EVENTS . . .	1. Fall. 2. Promise of Redemption. 3. Deluge.	1. Dispersion. 2. Jour. of the Patriarchs. 3. Exp. in Egypt.	1. Exp. in the Wild. 2. Conq. of Canaan. 3. Rule of the Judges	1. Saul's Def. 2. Ark removed. 3. Temple built.	1. Division. 2. Decay.	1. Chaldean Rule. 2. Persian Rule. 3. Greek Rule. 4. Maccab. Freedom. 5. Roman Rule.
INSTITUTIONS .		ALTAR.	TABERNACLE.		TEMPLE.	SYNAGOGUE.
DATES		2348	1491	1095 or 1037	975 or 937	587
DISPENSATIONS	PATRIARCHAL.		J E W I S H			

NOTE.—Practice on this chart until you can repeat with ease the sixteen persons, six periods, the different events or epochs in the various periods, and the five dates. By means of this chart you can answer many of the "Drill Questions" on Old Testament history. After studying Lesson XVI. return to this chart and fill in the dispensations; and after studying Lessons XXIII., XXIV. and XXV., fill in the institutions.

PART IV.

SIX LESSONS ON NEW TESTAMENT HISTORY

LESSON XII. THE LIFE OF CHRIST BY PERIODS

The New Testament history naturally falls into three divisions:
I. The Life of Christ.
II. Beginnings of the Church.
III. The Life of Paul.
The first division extends from B. C. 4 to A. D. 30.
The second period extends from A. D. 30 to about A. D. 37.
The third period extends from A. D. 37 to A. D. 67.

I. **The Life of Christ.**—The life of Christ may be divided into seven periods. These are: **Preparation, First Year, Second Year, Third Year, Last Three Months, Last Week, Forty Days.**

1. **Preparation.**—The period of **Preparation** extends from Christ's birth to the beginning of his ministry. Five of the most important events in this period were:

(1) **Birth.**—Jesus was born in Bethlehem of Judea in the days of Herod the king (Matt. 2: 1).

(2) **Flight.**—Soon after Jesus was born he was taken by the direction of Jehovah to Egypt in order to escape King Herod (Matt. 2: 13-15).

(3) **Return.**—After Herod died, Jesus was brought back to Nazareth, where he remained until he was about thirty years of age (Matt. 2: 19-23; Luke 2: 39).

(4) **Baptism.**—When Jesus was about thirty years of age, John the Baptist was baptizing in the Jordan River. Among others who came to be baptized, was Jesus (Matt. 3: 13-17; Mark 1: 9-11; Luke 3: 21-23).

(5) **Temptation.**—Following Christ's baptism, he was led away into the wilderness and was tempted (Matt. 4: 1-11; Mark 1: 12, 13; Luke 4: 1-13).

2. **First Year.**—The **first year** of Christ's ministry was the second period in his life. This is familiarly called the year of obscurity. In this we name five events:

(1) **First Miracle.**—In Cana of Galilee, Christ performed his first miracle, which was that of turning water into wine (John 2: 1-11).

(2) **First Cleansing.**—During this period of his life Christ cleansed the temple in Jerusalem, which he cleansed again on Monday before the crucifixion (John 2: 13-25; Matt. 21: 12-17).

(3) **Nicodemus.**—One of the most familiar characters in the New Testament is that of Nicodemus, the man who came to Jesus by night and said, "Rabbi, we know that thou art a teacher come from God: for no man can do these signs that thou doest except God be with him" (John 3: 2). Christ's first recorded discourse was with Nicodemus (John 3: 1-21).

(4) **Woman of Samaria.**—Jesus talked to the woman of Samaria at Jacob's well concerning the things of eternal life (John 4: 1-42).

(5) **Nobleman's Son.**—Christ healed the nobleman's son without going where the son was (John 4: 43-54).

3. **Second Year.**—The third period of the life of Christ was the second year of his ministry. This is often called the year of popularity. For the events of the first year of Christ's ministry, we turn to John's record. For those of the second year, we are obliged to refer to the synoptic Gospels. In the latter many more are recorded than in the former year, five of which we name:

(1) **Calling Fishers.**—By the Lake of Galilee Christ called some disciples to be fishers of men (Matt. 4: 18-22; Mark 1: 14-20; Luke 5: 1-11).

(2) **Sermon on the Mount.**—This sermon is given in detail in Matt. 5-7.

(3) **Widow's Son.**—Christ raised the widow's son from the dead, just outside of the city of Nain (Luke 7: 11-17).

(4) **Lakeside Parables.**—By the Lake of Galilee near Capernaum, Jesus spoke eight parables (Matt. 13: 1-53; Mark 4: 1-34; Luke 8: 1-15).

(5) **Jairus' Daughter.**—Christ raised the daughter of Jairus in the city of Capernaum (Matt. 9: 18-26; Mark 5: 21-43; Luke 8: 40-56).

BLACKBOARD WORK.

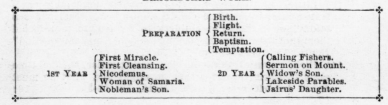

	PREPARATION	Birth. Flight. Return. Baptism. Temptation.	
1ST YEAR	First Miracle. First Cleansing. Nicodemus. Woman of Samaria. Nobleman's Son.	2D YEAR	Calling Fishers. Sermon on Mount. Widow's Son. Lakeside Parables. Jairus' Daughter.

TEST QUESTIONS.

1. Name the three periods of New Testament history.
2. Give the extent of each period.
3. Name seven periods in the life of Christ.
4. Name five events in the period of Preparation.
5. Name five events in the First Year.
6. What is this year often called?
7. Name five events in the Second Year.
8. What is this year often called?
9. Name in order fifteen events in the first three periods in Christ's life.

LESSON XIII.   THE LIFE OF CHRIST BY PERIODS (Concluded)

The three periods in the life of Christ mentioned in our last lesson were **Preparation, First Year** and **Second Year**. The next period is:

4. **Third Year.**—This year is sometimes called the year of opposition. Five events in the third year of Christ's ministry are.

(1) **Feeding Five Thousand.**—Near the Lake of Galilee, Jesus fed five thousand with five loaves and two fishes. This miracle is recorded by all the Gospel writers (Matt. 14: 13-21; Mark 6: 30-44; Luke 9: 12-17; John 6: 1-13).

(2) **Syrophœnician Daughter.**—At the request of her mother, Jesus healed the daughter of the Syrophœnician woman (Matt. 15: 21-28; Mark 7: 24-30).

(3) **Peter's Confession.**—There is no more important statement in the Bible than that of Peter's confession recorded in Matt. 16: 13-28; Mark 8: 27-9: 1; Luke 9: 20.

(4) **Transfiguration.**—Following closely upon Peter's confession of Christ as the Son of God, Jesus goes up on Mount Hermon and is there transfigured (Matt. 17: 1-13; Mark 9: 2-13; Luke 9: 28-36).

(5) **Good Samaritan.**—The parable of the good Samaritan is recorded only by Luke (Luke 10: 23-37).

5. **Last Three Months.**—The **Fifth Period** in the life of Christ is the **last three months of his ministry.** Five events in this period are:

(1) **Lazarus.**—Christ raised Lazarus from the dead at Bethany, near Jerusalem (John 11: 1-46).

(2) **Ten Lepers.**—Jesus healed ten lepers, and only one came back to thank him (Luke 17: 11-19).

(3) **Little Children.**—While Christ was in Perea, he manifested interest in little children. On one occasion Jesus said, "Suffer the little children to come unto me; forbid them not: for to such belongeth the kingdom of God" (Matt. 19. 13-15; Luke 18: 15-17).

(4) **Rich Young Ruler.**—A rich young ruler at one time came to Christ in order that he might find what he must do to inherit eternal life (Matt. 19: 16-30; Mark 10: 17-31; Luke 18: 18-30).

(5) **Zaccheus.**—The little man who climbed up a tree to see Jesus and who afterward entertained Jesus in his home (Luke 19: 1-10).

6. Last Week.—The **Sixth Period** of the life of Christ is the last week of his ministry. In this period we mention five events:

(1) **Mary's Anointing.**—On Saturday evening Mary anointed Jesus at Bethany (Matt. 26: 6-13; Mark 14: 3-9; John 12: 1-11).

(2) **Triumphal Entry.**—Christ's triumphal entry into Jerusalem was on Sunday before the crucifixion (Matt. 21: 1-11; Mark 11: 1-11; Luke 19: 29-44; John 12: 12-19).

(3) **The Ten Virgins.**—Christ gave the parable of the ten virgins, on Tuesday before the crucifixion (Matt. 25: 1-13).

(4) **Upper Room.**—In an upper room in Jerusalem Jesus met with his disciples, where he washed their feet and instituted the Lord's Supper (Matt. 26: 17-29; Mark 14: 12-25; Luke 22: 7-38; John 13: 1-17: 26).

(5) **Crucifixion.**—Jesus was crucified on Friday, April 7, A. D. 30 (Matt. 27: 35-56; Mark 15: 24-41; Luke 23: 26-49; John 19: 16-37).

7. Forty Days.—The **Seventh Period** of Christ's life was the forty days after the resurrection. During these forty days he appeared ten or eleven times. Five of the most important appearances we here mention:

(1) **Appearance to Two.**—Christ appeared to two disciples while on their way to Emmaus (Mark 16: 12, 13; Luke 24: 13-35).

(2) **Appearance to Ten.**—In Jerusalem Christ appeared to all of the apostles except Thomas (Luke 24: 36-48; John 20: 19-23; 1 Cor. 15: 5).

(3) **Appearance to Seven.**—At the Lake of Galilee, Christ appeared to seven (John 21: 1-14).

(4) **Appearance to Five Hundred.**—In 1 Cor. 15: 6, Paul tells us that Christ appeared in Galilee to over five hundred.

(5) **Appearance to Eleven.**—On the Mount of Olives, at the time of Christ's ascension, he appeared to the eleven apostles (Luke 24: 50; Acts 1: 1-8).

BLACKBOARD WORK.

For blackboard work, make, in the presence of the class, the chart found on page 32. Have each member of the class, some time before your next meeting, draw this chart from memory and hand it to you for correction.

TEST QUESTIONS.

1. Name seven periods in the life of Christ.
2. Name fifteen events in order in the first three periods.
3. Name five events in the Third Year of Christ's ministry.
4. What great miracle is recorded by all of the Gospel writers?

5. What Gospel writer gives the parable of the "Good Samaritan"?
6. Name five events in the Last Three Months of Christ's ministry.
7. What man climbed up a tree to see Christ?
8. Name five events in the Last Week of Christ's ministry.
9. On what day of the week did Christ make his triumphal entry into Jerusalem?
10. In what city was the memorable "upper room"?
11. What ordinance of the church was instituted in that room?
12. Name five appearances in the Forty Days following the resurrection.
13. How many apostles were present at the ascension?
14. Name thirty-five events in order in the life of Christ.

CHART OF THE LIFE OF CHRIST

PERIODS.	EVENTS.
PREPARATION (*Preparation*)* . .	BIRTH. FLIGHT. RETURN. BAPTISM. TEMPTATION.
FIRST YEAR (*Obscurity*)	FIRST MIRACLE. FIRST CLEANSING. NICODEMUS. WOMAN OF SAMARIA. NOBLEMAN'S SON.
SECOND YEAR (*Popularity*) . . .	CALLING FISHERS. SERMON ON THE MOUNT. WIDOW'S SON. LAKESIDE PARABLES. JAIRUS' DAUGHTER.
THIRD YEAR (*Opposition*	FEEDING FIVE THOUSAND. SYROPHŒNICIAN DAUGHTER. PETER'S CONFESSION. TRANSFIGURATION. GOOD SAMARITAN.
LAST THREE MONTHS 　　　　　(*Persecution*)	LAZARUS. TEN LEPERS. LITTLE CHILDREN. RICH YOUNG RULER. ZACCHEUS.
LAST WEEK (*Passion Week*) . . .	MARY'S ANOINTING. TRIUMPHAL ENTRY. TEN VIRGINS. UPPER ROOM. CRUCIFIXION.
FORTY DAYS (*Resurrection Days*) .	APPEARANCE TO TWO. APPEARANCE TO TEN. APPEARANCE TO SEVEN. APPEARANCE TO FIVE HUNDRED. APPEARANCE TO ELEVEN.

NOTE.—Practice on this chart till you can repeat the seven periods and thirty-five events with absolute ease. Use it continuously in your teaching, as it will help you to keep in mind in a systematic way all the events of Christ's life. Make out this chart from memory, and then answer from it No. 125 in the "Drill Questions."
　*The words in italics after the names of the periods are meant to characterize the periods.

LESSON XIV. BEGINNINGS OF THE CHURCH

After the ascension of Christ, his apostles returned from the Mount of Olives to Jerusalem, where they tarried until the day of Pentecost. This lesson naturally divides itself into two periods:

I. Church at Jerusalem.

II. Church Outside of Jerusalem.

I. Church at Jerusalem.—We mention five events under this heading. They are given in one word each to aid the memory, and enable the teacher to drill the class in concert upon them.

1. Pentecost.—Christ said in the sixteenth chapter of Matthew that he would build a church. This church, however, did not begin until after his death, resurrection and ascension. Its door was thrown open on the day of Pentecost, ten days after the ascension (Acts 2: 1-47).

2. Persecution.—No sooner had the disciples begun to preach than they began to meet opposition. This opposition went to the extent of persecution, in which all the apostles met death but John (Acts 4: 1-31; 5: 17-41).

3. Hypocrites.—In the last part of the fourth chapter of Acts, we are told how the early disciples had all things in common. All their possessions were given over to the apostles and distributed to each according as any one had need. This perfect harmony, however, did not exist long because of two professed disciples who turned out to be hypocrites. These were Ananias and Sapphira (Acts 5: 1-16).

4. Deacons.—When the disciples began to multiply, there was some murmuring because the widows were neglected in the daily ministrations. To do this work, seven deacons were chosen, of whom Stephen and Philip were the greatest (Acts 6: 1-6).

5. Stephen.—Stephen had not been long in his labors for Christ before he began to meet opposition. This opposition finally culminated in his death (Acts 6: 8-15; 7: 1-60).

II. Church Outside of Jerusalem.—Many of the events connected with the spread of the early church may be associated with Philip, Peter and Paul.

1. Labors of Philip.—When the disciples were scattered abroad because of the persecution, Philip went to the city of Samaria (Acts 8: 4-23); and then, through divine direction, went on toward Gaza, where he was the means of converting the Ethiopian eunuch (Acts 8: 26-40).

2. Labors of Peter.—Peter, who is called the "rock apostle," was a central figure in the early church. Many events may be connected with this man. With John he toured Samaria, at Lydda he healed Æneas, at Joppa he raised Tabitha from the dead (Acts 8: 14-25; 9: 32-43), but the event that we must note especially just now in connection with the labors of Peter is the conversion of Cornelius. In Cæsarea, there was a man whose name was Cornelius, who feared God, gave much alms to the people and prayed to God always. Through Peter this man became a disciple of Christ. As

Cornelius was a Gentile, his conversion opened the door of the church to the Gentiles (Acts 10: 1-44; 11: 1-18).

NOTE.—The student will see why we headed this chapter "Beginnings" rather than "Beginning" of the church. The church for the Jews began on the day of Pentecost, but for those who were not Jews, it began at the conversion of Cornelius.

3. **Conversion of Paul.**—When Stephen was stoned, Paul consented unto his death. Afterwards, we find him securing letters from the high priest to go down to Damascus to persecute the Christians. While on his way from Jerusalem to Damascus, he was turned from a pitiless persecutor to a chosen saint (Acts 9: 1-30).

BLACKBOARD WORK.

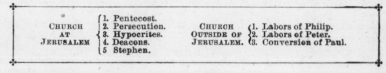

| CHURCH AT JERUSALEM | 1. Pentecost. 2. Persecution. 3. Hypocrites. 4. Deacons. 5 Stephen. | CHURCH OUTSIDE OF JERUSALEM. | 1. Labors of Philip. 2. Labors of Peter. 3. Conversion of Paul. |

TEST QUESTIONS.

1. Name the three divisions of New Testament history.
2. Name the two periods of the "Beginnings of the Church."
3. Name five events connected with the church at Jerusalem.
4. Name two hypocrites in the early church.
5. Name two of the seven deacons.
6. How did Stephen meet his death?
7. Name three men connected with the spread of the early church outside of Jerusalem.
8. Who was Cornelius?
9. Why is his conversion significant?
10. From what city to what city was Paul going when he was converted?

LESSON XV. THE LIFE OF PAUL BY PERIODS

Our last lesson gives us the connecting links between Christ's ascension and the conversion of Paul. Having now in a general way studied the beginnings of the church, first among the Jews and then among the Gentiles, we are ready to take an outline sketch of the apostle Paul, the man who was chosen as a special messenger of Christ to the Gentiles. We know very little in detail concerning Paul's life, but we have enough to show what manner of life he lived and what manner of man he was.

In Paul's life we make six periods. Some of these periods overlap each other, but they are nevertheless distinct.

I. **Paul the Student.**—This period of his life was spent in two cities.

1. **In Tarsus.**—Paul was born in Tarsus of Cilicia, where he spent the early years of his life. Like all Jewish boys, he learned a trade, which in his case was tentmaking (Acts 22: 3).

2. **In Jerusalem.**—In his early teens, Paul went to the city of Jerusalem, where he was instructed by Gamaliel (Acts 22: 3).

II. **Paul the Persecutor.**—Under this heading we note two events:

1. **Stoning of Stephen.**—While a student in Jerusalem, Paul witnessed the stoning of Stephen. Just how much Paul had a part in this we do not know. He at least consented unto his death (Acts 7: 58; 26: 10).

2. **Trip to Damascus.**—So earnestly did Paul persecute the Christians that he was not willing to stay in Jerusalem, but, after receiving letters from the high priest at Jerusalem, he went to Damascus to persecute them (Acts 9: 1, 2; 22: 4, 5; 26: 11, 12).

III. **Paul the Convert.**—Paul was on his way from Jerusalem to Damascus to persecute the Christians when he was turned from a pitiless persecutor to a chosen saint. Under his conversion we note:

1. **Experience on the Way.**—Before Paul reached Damascus, the Lord appeared to him and convinced him that he was Jesus of Nazareth whom he was persecuting (Acts 9: 1-8; 22: 5-11; 26: 12-18).

2. **Experience in Damascus.**—Here Paul was blind for three days; at the end of this period Ananias came to him and told him that he was to be a chosen vessel unto the Lord, to bear his name before the Gentiles and kings and children of Israel. Ananias told him to arise and be baptized (Acts 9: 9-18; 22: 12-16).

IV. **Paul the Missionary.**—Paul made three great missionary tours:

1. **First Missionary Journey.**—This was from Antioch through Asia Minor back to Antioch (Acts 13-15).

2. **Second Missionary Journey.**—This was not only through Asia Minor, but Paul, on his second tour, went on over into Europe (Acts 15-18).

3. **Third Missionary Journey.**—Paul's third missionary journey covered in a general way the same territory as his second (Acts 18-21).

Between his missionary journeys and following them, Paul made journeys to Jerusalem.

V. **Paul the Author.**

1. **Letters to Churches.**—These are Romans, 1 and 2 Corinthians, Galatians, Ephesians, Philippians, Colossians, 1 and 2 Thessalonians.

2. **Letters to Individuals.**—These are 1 and 2 Timothy, Titus and Philemon. Paul may have written the Hebrew letter. It is attributed to him by many because it is Pauline in character.

VI. **Paul the Prisoner.**

1. **In Caesarea.**—While on his last journey to Jerusalem, Paul was arrested and taken to Cæsarea and placed in prison. Here he spent two years (Acts 23-26).

2. **In Rome.**—Paul was taken from Cæsarea to Rome, where he was imprisoned, and where he finally met his death under the reign of Nero (Acts 27, 28).

BLACKBOARD WORK.

I. Student: In Ta. In Jer.
II. Persecutor: St. of St., Tr. to Da.
III. Convert: En. on the Wa., Ex. in Da.
IV. Missionary: Three Journeys.
V. Author: Le. to Ch., Le. to Ind.
VI. Prisoner: In Ca., in Ro.

TEST QUESTIONS.

1. Name the three divisions of New Testament history
2. Name six periods in the life of Paul.
3. In what two cities was he a student?
4. Describe Paul's conversion.
5. How many missionary journeys did he make?
6. Name the letters he wrote to churches.
7. Name the letters he wrote to individuals.
8. Name two cities in which Paul was a prisoner.
9. Under whose reign did Paul meet his death?

Seven Mile-posts in Paul's Life.

Conversion ....A. D. 37
Beginning of First Missionary Journey................A. D. 46
Beginning of Second Missionary Journey..............A. D. 51
Beginning of Third Missionary Journey...............A. D. 54
Arrest in Jerusalem and Imprisonment in Cæsarea......A. D. 58
Journey to Rome......................................A. D. 60
Death ....A. D. 67

LESSON XVI.   BIBLE HISTORY BY DISPENSATIONS*

We have arranged the Old Testament history in six divisions, and the New Testament history in three. We have divided the life of Christ into seven periods, the "'Beginnings of the Church" into two, and the life of Paul into six. We are now ready to divide the whole Bible history into dispensations. Of these there are three:

I. **Patriarchal Dispensation.**—This began with Adam and ended with the giving of the law at Mount Sinai. The institution of worship during this administration was the **Altar.**

II. **Jewish Dispensation.**—This began with the giving of the law at Mount Sinai and ended with the death of Christ. The three institutions of worship during this period were the **Tabernacle,** the **Temple** and the **Synagogue.** The tabernacle began with Moses, the temple with Solomon, and the synagogue with Ezra. While the children of Israel were wandering in the wilderness, it was

---

*This lesson does not wholly belong to those on New Testament history, but it naturally comes after a study of both the history of the Old and the New Testaments. It will therefore be proper to study the dispensations of Bible history at this point. Classes that find this lesson too short should take Lesson XVII. together with this one.

necessary for them to have a portable house of worship. The tabernacle answered for this. When the people were finally settled in Canaan, a more stable building for worship was desired. To answer this desire, a temple was finally erected. This temple was destroyed at the time of the Babylonian captivity. The worship of Jehovah, however, continued during the captivity, with the result that the synagogue had its beginning. Synagogues existed all through the comparatively silent years between the Old and New Testament history, and at the coming of Christ they were scattered everywhere.

III. **Christian Dispensation.**—The life and work of Christ laid the foundation for a new dispensation. When the **Christian dispensation** began, the synagogue gave way to the **church.** We to-day are living under the **Christian dispensation.**

BLACKBOARD WORK.

I. PATRIARCHAL DISPENSATION—Altar.
II. JEWISH DISPENSATION—Tabernacle, Temple, Synagogue.
III. CHRISTIAN DISPENSATION—Church.

TEST QUESTIONS.

1. Name the six divisions of Old Testament history.
2. Name the three divisions of New Testament history.
3. Name the three dispensations of Bible history.
4. Give the extent of the patriarchal dispensation; of the Jewish; of the Christian.
5. What were the institutions of worship under each?
6. Under which dispensation are we living?

LESSON XVII. REVIEW OF NEW TESTAMENT HISTORY

For your review use the "Drill Questions" in the back of the book. Review especially Questions 90 to 153, inclusive.

PART V.

FIVE LESSONS ON BIBLE GEOGRAPHY

LESSON XVIII.   THE OLD TESTAMENT WORLD.
LESSON XIX.   THE NEW TESTAMENT WORLD.
LESSON XX.   THE LAND OF PALESTINE.
LESSON XXI.   THE WHOLE BIBLE WORLD.
LESSON XXII.   REVIEW OF BIBLE GEOGRAPHY.

LESSON XVIII. THE OLD TESTAMENT WORLD

In studying the Old Testament world, read carefully these questions and answers, comparing each answer with the map. Go over the questions a second time, using a card to conceal the answers, and answer them by looking at the map. Then hand somebody the book and have him ask you the questions, and you answer them from memory; then from memory ask and answer the questions. Study the map until you have it indelibly drawn on your memory.

1. What is the great sea of Bible geography? *Mediterranean.*

2. What country is located southeast of the Mediterranean Sea? *Canaan.*

3. What do we call the little strip of land directly north of Canaan? *Phœnicia.*

4. What country is directly east of Phœnicia? *Syria.*

5. What country is northeast of Syria? *Mesopotamia.*

6. What does the word "Mesopotamia" mean? *Between rivers.*

7. What rivers is Mesopotamia between? *Euphrates and Tigris Rivers.*

8. In what general direction does the Euphrates River flow? *Southeast.*

9. Into what does the Euphrates River empty? *Persian Gulf.*

10. What general direction does the Tigris River flow? *Southeast.*

11. Into what does the Tigris River flow? *Into the Euphrates River, near the Persian Gulf.*

12. What country is east of Mesopotamia? *Assyria.*

13. What country is east of Assyria? *Media.*

14. What country is north of Assyria? *Armenia.*

15. What country is southeast of Assyria? *Elam*

38

16. What country is southwest of Elam? *Chaldea.*

17. What country is east of Elam? *Persia.*

18. What great desert lies between Canaan and Chaldea? *Arabia.*

19. What country lies south of Canaan? *The Wilderness.*

20. What continent is southwest of the Wilderness? *Africa.*

21. What great Bible land is in Africa? *Egypt.*

22. What sea is in the northwestern corner of the Old Testament world? *Black Sea.*

23. What sea is in the northeastern corner of the Old Testament world? *Caspian Sea.*

24. What gulf is in the southeastern corner of the Old Testament world? *Persian Gulf.*

25. What sea is in the southwestern corner of the Old Testament world? *Red Sea.*

26. What sea is in Canaan? *Dead Sea.*

27. What lake is in Canaan? *Lake of Galilee.*

28. What river connects the Lake of Galilee with the Dead Sea? *Jordan.*

29. What is the great river of Egypt? *Nile.*

30. On what mountain did the Ark rest? *Ararat.*

31. What range of mountains goes around the southern end of the Caspian Sea? *Caspian.*

32. What range of mountains parallels the Tigris River? *Zagros.*

33. What range of mountains runs north of Paul's home? *Taurus.*

34. What range of mountains runs down through Canaan? *Lebanon.*

BLACKBOARD WORK.

SEAS	MOUNTAIN RANGES
1. Caspian. 2. Persian Gulf. 3. Red. 4. Dead. 5. Galilee (Lake). 6. Mediterranean.	1. Caspian. 2. Zagros. 3. Lebanon. 4. Taurus.

RIVERS	LANDS	
1. Nile. 2. Euphrates. 3. Jordan.	1. Arm. 2. Med. 3. Per. 4. Mes. 5. Chal. 6. El.	7. Assy. 8. Phœ. 9. Sy. 10. Ca. 11. Wi. 12. Eg.

TEST QUESTIONS.

1. Give the approximate length and breadth of the Old Testament world.
2. Name and locate four seas.
3. Name and locate four mountain ranges.
4. Name and locate three rivers.
5. Name and locate six Old Testament lands.

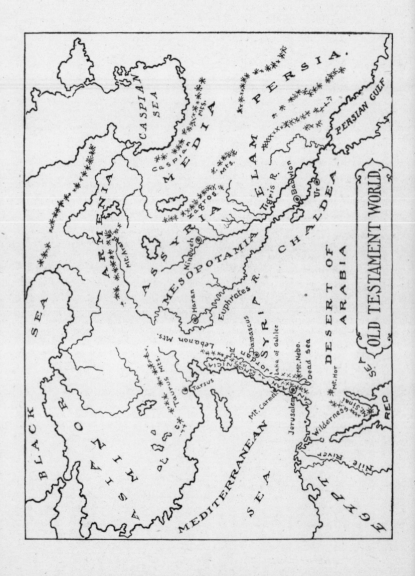

LESSON XIX. THE NEW TESTAMENT WORLD*

I. **Continents of the New Testament World.**

The New Testament world covers a part of the three continents Africa, Asia and Europe.

1. **Bible Lands in Africa.**

(1) **Egypt,** south of the eastern end of the Mediterranean Sea.

(2) **Libya,** directly east of Egypt.

2. **Bible Lands in Europe.**

(1) **Italy,** the boot-shaped country in the northwestern corner of the map of the New Testament world.

(2) **Greece,** directly east of the southern end of Italy.

(3) **Macedonia,** north of Greece.

(4) **Thrace,** east of Macedonia.

(5) **Illyricum,** west of Macedonia.

3. **Bible Lands in Asia.**

(1) **Canaan,** southeast of the Mediterranean Sea.

(2) **Phoenicia,** a little strip of land directly north of Canaan.

(3) **Syria,** a large country east of Phœnicia.

(4) **Asia Minor,** directly north of the eastern end of the Mediterranean Sea.

II. **Seas of the New Testament World.**

1. **Black Sea,** north of Asia Minor.

2. **Mediterranean Sea,** the great sea of the Bible world, washing the shores of Europe, Asia and Africa.

3. **Aegean Sea,** between Asia Minor and Greece.

4. **Adriatic Sea,** east of Italy.

5. **Sicilian Sea,** east of Sicily.

6. **Dead Sea,** at the southern end of Palestine.

7. **Sea of Galilee,** in the northern part of Palestine.

III. **Islands of the New Testament World.**

1. **Cyprus,** in the northeastern corner of the Mediterranean Sea.

2. **Patmos,** in the Ægean Sea near Ephesus.

3. **Crete,** in the Mediterranean Sea south of the Ægean Sea.

4. **Sicily,** south of Italy.

5. **Melita,** south of Sicily.

IV. **Provinces of Asia Minor.**—For convenience in memorizing them, we divide them into three groups:

(1) The three that begin with C:

Caria.

Cilicia (Acts 21: 39).

Cappadocia (Acts 2: 9).

(2) The three that begin with L:

Lydia.

Lycia.

Lycaonia (Acts 14: 6).

(3) The five that begin with P:

Pontus (Acts 18: 2).

---

*In studying this lesson use the map on page 43. Compare this map with the one on page 40 to see how the map has moved westward.

Paphlagonia.
Pisidia (Acts 13: 14).
Phrygia (Acts 16: 6).
Pamphylia (Acts 13: 13).
(4) The remainder:
Bithynia (1 Pet. 1: 1).
Mysia.
Galatia.

BLACKBOARD WORK.

				PROVINCES IN EUROPE, AFRICA AND ASIA			
SEAS	1. Bl. / 2. Æ. / 3. Ad.	ISLANDS	1. Cy. / 2. Pa. / 3. Cr. / 4. Si. / 5. Me.	EU	1. Th. / 2. Ma. / 3. Ill. / 4. Gr. / 5. It.	AF.	1. Li. / 2. Eg.
						AS.	1. Ju. / 2. Ph. / 3. Ar.
ASIA MINOR	C. Ca. / Ci. / Ca.	L. Lyd. / Lyc. / Lyca.		P. Po. / Pa. / Pi. / Ph. / Pa.	OTHERS Bi. / My. / Ga.		

TEST QUESTIONS.*

1. Locate the following seas: Black, Ægean, Adriatic.
2. Name five islands in the New Testament world.
3. Name two provinces in each of the following continents: (1) Europe; (2) Africa; (3) Asia.
4. In what provinces of Asia Minor are the following cities: (1) Tarsus; (2) Troas; (3) Ephesus?
5. Name the provinces of Asia Minor bordering on the Mediterranean Sea. On the Ægean Sea.

LESSON XX. THE LAND OF PALESTINE

I. **Its Names.**

1. **Canaan.**—This word means "lowland," and refers only to the section between the river Jordan and the Mediterranean Sea, of which the best-known inhabitants were Canaanites, dwelling in the lowland plain (Gen. 12: 5).

2. **Israel.**—A name by which it was known after its conquest by Joshua.

3. **Judea.**—This was its political name after the Babylonian captivity. Its most important province also bore this name (Mark 1: 5).

4. **Palestine.**—A name by which this land has been known since the time of Christ. It is a form of the word "Philistine," the name of a race which at one time occupied its southwest border (Isa. 14: 29).

II. **Its Dimensions.**

---

*It will not be necessary for the student to memorize all of the provinces of Asia Minor. Answers to the test questions will be sufficient.

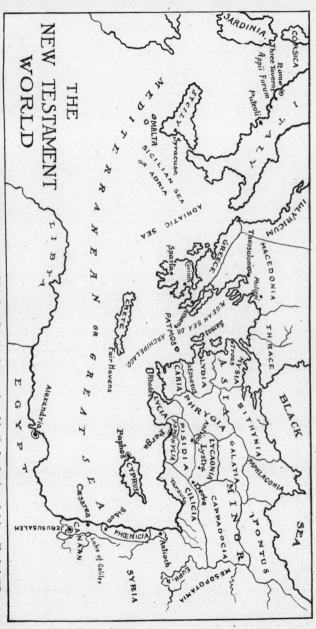

THE
NEW TESTAMENT
WORLD

This map and the lesson on the New Testament World is based upon the map found in the beginning of Adam Clarke's "Commentary and Critical Notes on the New Testament." While it was published in 1847, it is clear and accurate. The only country that is added is Illyricum, the country lying west of Macedonia. Most of the cities have been left off, as the purpose of this map is to give the bold outline rather than the minute details.

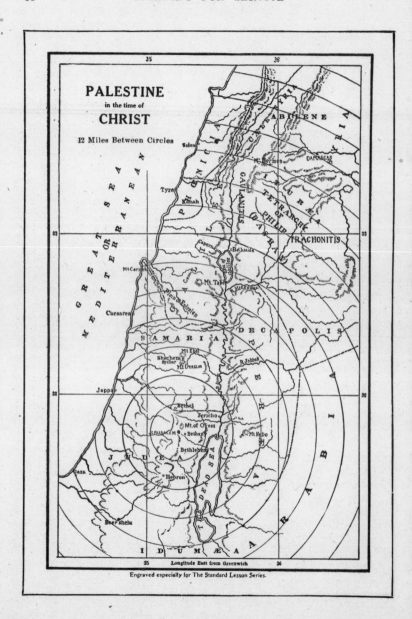

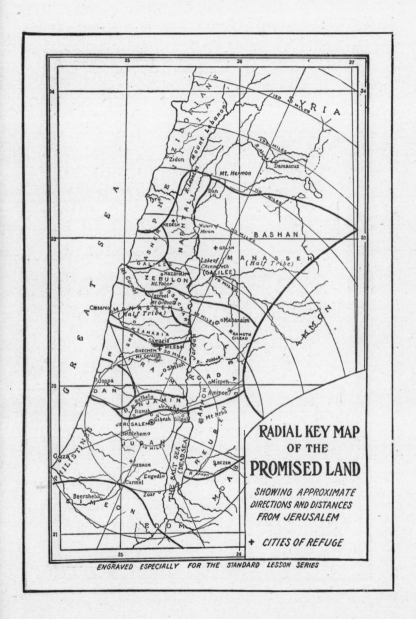

RADIAL KEY MAP
OF THE
PROMISED LAND

SHOWING APPROXIMATE
DIRECTIONS AND DISTANCES
FROM JERUSALEM

+ CITIES OF REFUGE

ENGRAVED ESPECIALLY FOR THE STANDARD LESSON SERIES

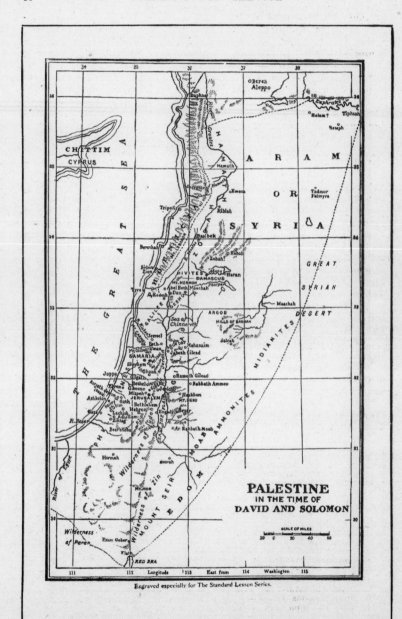

PALESTINE
IN THE TIME OF
DAVID AND SOLOMON

SCALE OF MILES

Engraved especially for The Standard Lesson Series.

The entire length of the country "from Dan to Beer-sheba" is 139 miles in an air-line. Its width at the northern extremity is about thirty miles, and at the southern, about fifty miles. The whole area west of the Jordan is about six thousand square miles. The territory of the tribes which dwelt east of the Jordan was not so long nor wide. It extended from the river Arnon on the south, a stream which flows westward from the desert and enters the Dead Sea about midway its length, to a line drawn eastward from the northern end of the Lake of Galilee, a distance of about one hundred miles; and its average width is not more than twenty-five miles (*McGarvey*).

III. **Its Political Divisions.**—Palestine is divided into five political divisions: (1) Judea, (2) Samaria, (3) Galilee, (4) Perea, (5) Bashan. Bashan is generally referred to as "Philip's Tetrarchy" (Luke 3: 1), and is divided from Perea by the river Hieromax. See the map on page 44.

IV. **Its Natural Divisions.**—Passing across Palestine from west to east, we first strike a low level plain known as the *Maritime Plain*. Going on farther east, we come to the rising, rolling *foot-hills* of the mountains of Ephraim and Judah. This elevated region is called *Shephelah*. Crossing Shephelah, we come to a central range of *mountains* which form an elevated backbone 2,500 and 4,000 feet high. Having crossed the mountains, we next come to the *Jordan Valley*, with the vast *table-land* beyond.

V. **Its Seas.**—The Dead Sea lies in the southern end of Palestine, and the Mediterranean Sea washes its western coast. The Lake of Galilee and Lake Merom are in the northern part.

VI. **Its Inhabitants.**—The population of Palestine to-day consists largely of Turks, Jews and Arabs. Aside from these, there are a few from all quarters of the globe. The Arabs are divided very distinctly into two sects; the *Fellahin*, those who dwell in cities and villages; and the *Bedawin*, those who dwell in tents.

VII. **Its Chief City.**—Jerusalem. Situated thirty-two miles from the sea and eighteen miles from the Jordan. It occupies four hills: Zion, Acra, Moriah and the Bezetha.

BLACKBOARD WORK.

NAMES: Ca., Is., Ju., Pa., Ho., La.
DIMENSIONS: 139; 30; 50; 6,000; 100; 25.
POLITICAL DIVISIONS: Ju., Sa., Gal., Per., Ba.
NATURAL DIVISIONS: Ma., Ft., Mt., Jo., Ta.
ITS SEAS: De., Med., Gal., Mer.
ITS INHABITANTS: Tu., Je., Ar.
ITS CHIEF CITY: Je.—4 hills, Zi., Ac., Mo., Be.

TEST QUESTIONS.

1. Give the four names applied to the Holy Land
2. Give the dimensions of the Holy Land.
3. Name the five political divisions.
4. Name the natural divisions.
5. Name and locate the seas and lakes of Palestine.
6. What persons are the chief inhabitants of Palestine to-day?
7. Name the four hills on which Jerusalem is situated.

LESSON XXI. THE WHOLE BIBLE WORLD

BIBLE GEOGRAPHY SIMPLIFIED.

In teaching the location of the Bible rivers, mountains, cities and lakes, each student should make a map of his own. Make first simply the coast-lines, then fill in, as you go along, first the rivers (when the rivers are drawn, teach also the lakes or seas through which or into which they flow); then the mountains; then the cities.

Question. Name three Bible rivers.

Answer. Nile, Euphrates, Jordan.

Q. Name one event connected with the Nile River.

A. The birth of Moses (Ex. 2: 1-10).

Q. Name one event connected with the Euphrates River.

A. The captivity of the Jews.

Q. Name one event connected with the Jordan River.

A. The baptism of Jesus (Matt. 3: 13-17).

Q. Name five Bible mountains.

A. Sinai, Nebo, Carmel, Hermon, Olives.

Q. What event is connected with Mt. Sinai?

A. The giving of the Law (Ex. 20, etc.).

Q. What event is connected with Mt. Nebo?

A. Moses' death (Deut. 34: 1-7).

Q. What event is connected with Mt. Carmel?

A. Elijah's sacrifice (1 Kings 18: 19-39).

Q. What event took place on Mt. Hermon?

A. The transfiguration of Jesus (Matt. 17: 2-9).

Q. What event took place on the Mount of Olives?

A. The ascension of Christ (Acts 1: 9-11).

Q. Name three Bible cities that begin with B.

A. Babylon, Bethlehem, Bethany.

Q. Name one event connected with Babylon.

A. Daniel in the lions' den (Dan. 6).

Q. What event is connected with Bethlehem?

A. The birth of Christ (Matt. 1: 18-25).

Q. What man, who was a close friend of Christ's, lived in Bethany?

A. Lazarus (John 11: 1).

Q. Name three Bible cities that begin with C.

A. Cana, Capernaum, Corinth.

Q. What event is connected with Cana?

A. Christ's first miracle (John 2: 1-11).

Q. What makes Capernaum of great importance?

A. Christ's home during his Galilean ministry.

Q. What two letters in the New Testament did Paul write to the people at Corinth?

A. 1 and 2 Corinthians.

Q. Name three Bible cities that begin with J.

A. Jerusalem, Jericho, Joppa.

Q. Name one event associated with Jerusalem.

A. Christ's triumphal entry (Mark 11: 1-11).

Q. Name one man associated with Jericho.

A. Zaccheus (Luke 19: 1-10).

Q. What event is associated with Joppa?

A. Peter's vision concerning his duty to the Gentiles (Acts 10).

Q. Name three Bible cities that begin with T.

A. Tyre, Tarsus, Troas.

Q. What event in the life of Christ took place near Tyre?

A. Christ healed the Syrophœnician woman's daughter near Tyre (Matt. 15: 21-28).

Q. What important person was born in Tarsus?

A. Paul (Acts 21: 39).

Q. What event is connected with Troas?

A. At Troas Paul heard the Macedonian cry, "Come over into Macedonia and help us" (Acts 16: 9).

BLACKBOARD WORK.

RIVERS	1. Nile. 2. Euphrates. 3. Jordan.	MOUNTAINS	1. Sinai. 2. Nebo. 3. Carmel. 4. Hermon. 5. Olives.	CITIES	B. C. J. T. B. C. J. T. B. C. J. T.

TEST QUESTIONS.

1. Name and locate three Bible rivers.
2. Name and locate five Bible mountains.
3. Name and locate three cities that begin with B. With C. With J. With T.
4. Through what lake does the Jordan River flow?
5. In what sea is the Jordan River lost?
6. Into what sea does the Nile River flow?
7. Into what gulf does the Euphrates River flow?

NOTE.—In teaching this lesson use the map on page 50. Draw it upon the blackboard. This map gives something new in Bible geography in that it brings together the lands of both the Old and the New Testaments. The purpose in having the definite rivers, mountains and cities memorized and located is that they may be used as guideposts in locating all other places in Bible history. It is not necessary now to commit the events that are associated with the various rivers, mountains and cities. The one thing we want you to do now is to form in your mind a definite outline picture of the whole Bible world.

LESSON XXII.   REVIEW OF BIBLE GEOGRAPHY

For a review of Bible geography use Questions 154 to 185, inclusive, of the "Drill Questions." Review also the first 153 questions.

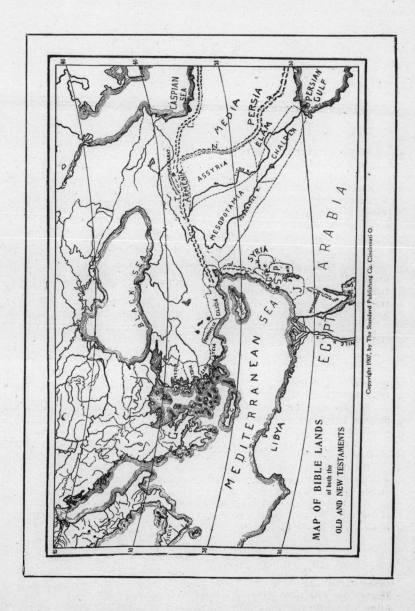

MAP OF BIBLE LANDS
of both the
OLD AND NEW TESTAMENTS

PART VI.

FIVE LESSONS ON OLD TESTAMENT INSTITUTIONS

LESSON XXIII. THE ALTAR AND THE TABERNACLE

In the history of the worship of Jehovah, previous to the beginning of the Christian dispensation, there were four great institutions, each related to some extent to the others and each fitted to the needs of the various periods. These institutions were: I. The Altar. II. The Tabernacle. III. The Temple. IV. The Synagogue.

In our lesson to-day we notice the first two of these religious institutions.

THE ALTAR.

I. The First Recorded Altar Service.—The first recorded altar service is in connection with the accepted offering of Abel and the rejected offering of Cain (Gen. 4: 3-7).

II. The General Use of the Altar.—In patriarchal times the worshipers built altars wherever they pitched their tents or had special occasion to sacrifice to the true God (Gen. 8: 20; 12: 7; 22: 9; 35: 1, 7; Ex. 17: 15; 24: 4). The altar was a meeting-place between God and man. Upon it the worshiper offered his sacrifice to Jehovah.

III. How the Altar was Made.—The material of which the altar was made might be a huge stone, or a mound of earth, or several stones placed one upon the other, or it might be made of metal.

IV. The Typical Meaning of the Altar.—The typical meaning of the altar is given in the discussion of the "Tabernacle," under the heading "Altar of Burnt-offering."

THE TABERNACLE.

1. Previous to the time when Moses led the Israelites out of the captivity in Egypt, the worship centered around the family altar. Beginning with the erection of the tabernacle, there was but one altar for all the twelve tribes.

2. At Mt. Sinai God gave directions for the building of the tabernacle, and thus the altar grew into the tabernacle (Ex. 25-40).

In considering the tabernacle, we will first take up its three different parts, giving the furnishings of the same and their meaning. Following this will be given the five different kinds of offerings, and the significance of the same.

I. **The Court.**—About the tabernacle was a court which measured 150 feet east and west by seventy-five feet north and south. As was necessary among the wandering people, the wall of this court, as well as all of the parts of the tabernacle, was constructed of material that could easily be taken apart and carried on the march through the wilderness. The court wall was a curtain made

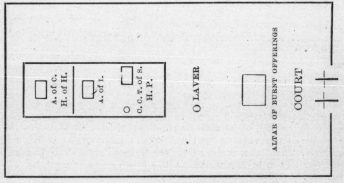

DIAGRAM SHOWING POSITION OF THE OBJECTS WITHIN THE TABERNACLE COURT.

of fine-twined linen which was hung on posts of acacia wood, which had silver tops and rested on copper bases, and were connected by silver rods. Both the doors of the court and of the tabernacle opened eastward. The court is a type of the world. In this court we find:

1. **Altar of Burnt-offering.**—This altar was seven and a half feet square and four and a half feet high. It was made of acacia planks covered with copper, and was filled with unhewn stone or earth. The different kinds of sacrifices that were offered upon this altar are given later in this lesson. This altar, taken in connection with the offering, was a type of Christ's sacrifice.

2. **Laver.**—The laver contained water for washing all sacrifices. The priests, passing to and fro from the Holy Place and the altar, bathed their hands and their feet at the laver. On the day of atonement the high priest had to bathe the entire person there before entering the Holy of Holies. The size is unknown, but it must have been quite large (Ex. 30 ff.). The laver is a type of Christian baptism.

II. **The Holy Place.**—The tabernacle itself stood just beyond the laver. It was forty-five feet long and fifteen feet wide. It was divided into two rooms. The first, or eastward one, called the Holy

Place, was thirty feet long by fifteen feet high and fifteen feet wide. The second, or westward room, called the Holy of Holies, was a cube fifteen feet in dimensions. The Holy Place is a type of the church. The furnishings in it were:

1. **Golden Candlestick.**—This stood on the left side of one entering the Holy Place. It had seven lamps: a central one, and three on the arms at each side. This is generally taken to be a type of the Bible (Ex. 25: 31-40).

2. **Table of Showbread.**—This was three feet long, twenty-seven inches high and eighteen inches wide. It was made of acacia wood, overlaid with pure gold. On it every seventh day the priest placed

twelve loaves of bread. The table of showbread is a type of the Lord's Supper (Ex. 37: 10-16).

3. **Altar of Incense.**—This was three feet high and eighteen inches square. It was hollow, made of wood, covered with gold. On it a golden bowl rested, in which were placed coals of fire from the altar of burnt-offering, on which incense was poured, thus filling the whole room with a sweet-smelling smoke. This altar, with its incense, is a type of prayer (Ex. 30 ff.).

III. **The Holy of Holies.**—This is a type of heaven. In this room there was but one piece of furniture. It was the

1. **Ark of the Covenant.**—This was three feet nine inches long, and two feet three inches in width and height. It was made of shittim-wood, and covered on the outside and inside with gold. It was covered with a lid of solid gold which was called the "mercy-

seat." On this lid stood two figures of the cherubim. Two rings were attached to the body of the ark on each side, through which poles were passed which were used in carrying the ark from place to place. "The ark of the covenant was so called because it contained two tables of the law of the covenant between God and Israel" (Ex. 25: 10 ff.). The contents of the ark, aside from the two tables of the law, were the pot of manna and Aaron's rod that budded. On the lid of the ark the high priest sprinkled the blood on the day of atonement (Ex. 25: 17 ff.; Heb. 9: 7). As the ark pertained to "that which is within the veil," we deem it best not to attempt to interpret its typical significance.

IV. **Offerings.**—Of the Old Testament offerings there were five: *Sin, Burnt, Trespass, Meal* and *Peace.* The order and significance as given by Prof. H. B. Hackett, in Smith's "Dictionary of the Bible," is (a) The Burnt-offering—Self-dedicatory. (b) The Meat-offering (unbloody) and the Peace-offering (bloody)—Eucharistic. (c) The Sin-offering and the Trespass-offering—Expiatory.

1. **Sin-offering.**—This offering expressed a desire to rid the life of sin and a means of *reconciliation* with God (Lev. 4: 3).

2. **Burnt-offering.**—This offering was accepted as an *atonement* for sin (Lev. 1: 2 ff.).

3. **Trespass-offering.**—This was for the *forgiveness* of an actual transgression (Lev. 5: 1 ff.).

4. **Meal-offering.**—This was an expression of *thanksgiving* (Lev. 2: 1 ff.). It is generally referred to as *Meat*-offering, but it was an offering of fruit or grain.

5. **Peace-offering.**—This was a sign of *communion* with God (Lev. 3: 1 ff.).

The five offerings, therefore, may be considered as an expression of (1) reconciliation, (2) atonement, (3) forgiveness, (4) thanksgiving, (5) communion. It is to be understood that these words do not exhaust the meaning of the offerings. They are given to aid the memory.

BLACKBOARD WORK.

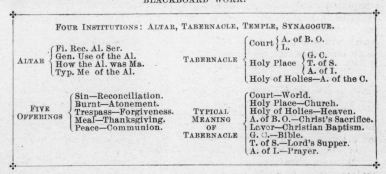

	FOUR INSTITUTIONS: ALTAR, TABERNACLE, TEMPLE, SYNAGOGUE.		
ALTAR	Fi. Rec. Al. Ser. Gen. Use of the Al. How the Al. was Ma. Typ. Me of the Al.	TABERNACLE	Court { A. of B. O. L. Holy Place { G. C. T. of S. A. of I. Holy of Holies—A. of the C.
FIVE OFFERINGS	Sin—Reconciliation. Burnt—Atonement. Trespass—Forgiveness. Meal—Thanksgiving. Peace—Communion.	TYPICAL MEANING OF TABERNACLE	Court—World. Holy Place—Church. Holy of Holies—Heaven. A. of B. O.—Christ's Sacrifice. Levor—Christian Baptism. G. C.—Bible. T. of S.—Lord's Supper. A. of I.—Prayer.

TEST QUESTIONS.

1. Name the four institutions of worship in the Old Testament.
2. What was the purpose of the altar?
3. Name the three different parts of the tabernacle.
4. What furnishings were in the court?
5. What furnishings were in the Holy Place? The Holy of Holies?
6. Give the typical meaning of the following: Court, Holy Place, Holy of Holies, Altar of Burnt-offering, Laver, Golden Candlestick, Table of Showbread, Altar of Incense.
7. Name the five kinds of offerings.
8. Name one thing that each offering expressed.

LESSON XXIV. THE TEMPLE

I. **The Reason for the Temple.**

1. **A Portable House of Worship.**—When the Israelites were in t' e wilderness they needed a portable house of worship. This was called the **Tabernacle**.

2. **A Permanent House of Worship.**—After the Israelites became settled in the land of Canaan and the kingdom had been thoroughly organized, a permanent house of worship was erected, called the **Temple**.

II. **The Three Temples.**

1. **Solomon's Temple.**—King David had much to do in making preparation for the building of the temple, yet it was left to his son Solomon to erect it. Solomon's temple was built about one thousand years before Christ.

2. **Zerubbabel's Temple.**—Solomon's temple was destroyed by Nebuchadnezzar, B. C. 587. After coming from the Babylonian captivity, Zerubbabel rebuilt the temple, completing it about B. C. 515.

3. **Herod's Temple.**—In the course of five hundred years this temple became dilapidated and was rebuilt and enlarged by Herod the Great, beginning about B. C. 20. This temple, however, was not completed until A. D. 65, just five years before its final destruction by Titus, a Roman general. While the three temples were built on the same general plan, we know most in detail about the last one, which was standing in the time of Christ. Its description will give us an understanding as well of the general plan of Solomon's temple.

III. **The Two Great Courts.**

1. **The Outer Court.**—The **Outer Court**, commonly called the court of the Gentiles, occupied the southern half of the temple area and entirely surrounded the courts within the Sacred Inclosure.

2. **The Inner Court.**—The **Inner Court** was a rectangle which included in it the women's court, the court of Israel, the court of the priests, and the temple proper.

IV. **The Six Departments of the Temple.**

The two great courts given above may be subdivided for convenience into six departments.

1. **Court of the Gentiles.**—This is called the **Court of the Gentiles** because the Gentiles were allowed to enter it. The walls of

this court were surrounded on the inside by porches, the most noted of which was on the south side, called **Solomon's Porch.** The entire **Court of the Gentiles** was paved with stone. This court was nearly square. "The exact measures are: 922 feet on the south, 1,090 feet on the east, 997 feet on the north and 1,138 feet on the west" (*Butler*). It was in this court where in Christ's time the money-changers were allowed to open up their treasures and the traders to put up their cattle for sale (Matt. 21: 12; John 2: 14).

2. **Sacred Inclosure.**—The inner court was on higher ground than the outer, there being five steps from the one to the other. Between the wall of the inner court and the porticoes of the outer court there was a free space of ten cubits, higher than the rest of the outer court, and reached by a flight of fourteen steps. This formed a terrace all round the inner court except the east, and was called the **hel** (pronounced **kel**) (*Davies*). Only those of the commonwealth of Israel were permitted within this **hel.**

3. **Court of the Women.**—Within the **Sacred Inclosure** are various courts. The one at the eastern end is called the **Court of the Women.** "This was a square of nearly 300 feet" (*Butler*). In each corner was a room used for various ceremonies and other purposes.

4. **Court of Israel.**—This court was west of the **Court of the Women,** and is commonly called the men's court. It is held by some to have only been on the east side of the court of the priests, but it very likely surrounded the entire court and was eleven cubits (sixteen feet) broad. Its length on the east and west side is the same as that of the **Court of the Women.**

5. **Court of the Priests.**—This court was regarded as more sacred than the **Court of Israel.** It entirely surrounded the temple proper. On the east side were the altar of burnt-offerings and the laver.

6. **The Temple Proper.**

Aside from the porch or vestibule in front, and chambers for the priests against the two sides and rear of the temple, we have the

(1) **Holy Place.**—This had twice the dimensions of the tabernacle. It was therefore thirty feet wide and sixty feet long. It contained the golden candlestick, the table of showbread and the altar of incense.

(2) **Holy of Holies.**—This was thirty feet on each side, being double that of the Holy of Holies of the tabernacle. It was separated from the Holy Place by a veil. This veil was rent at the death of Christ (Matt. 27: 51; Heb. 10: 20). There being no ark of the covenant at this time, the Holy of Holies contained only a block of marble upon which blood was sprinkled on the day of atonement.

BLACKBOARD WORK.

REASON	{ Port. Ho. of Wor. { Per. Ho. of Wor.	TWO GREAT COURTS	{ Outer Co. { Inner Co.
THREE TEMPLES	{ Sol. { Zerub. { Her.	DEPARTMENTS	1. Co. of the Ge. 2. Sa. In. 3. Co. of the Wo. 4. Co. of Is. 5. Co. of the Pr. 6. Te. Pro.

TEST QUESTIONS

1. What king did much in making preparation for the building of the temple?
2. Who built the first temple?
3. When was it destroyed?
4. Who rebuilt the temple?
5. What happened to it then?
6. Who rebuilt the temple again? When was it completed?
7. When and by whom was the temple finally destroyed?
8. Name the six departments of the temple.
9. In what period of Old Testament history was the first temple built? The second? The third?
10. What was allowed in the Court of the Gentiles in Christ's time?
11. Why was the Court of the Women so called?
12. What was in the Court of the Priests?
13. Give the furnishings in the Holy Place. The Holy of Holies

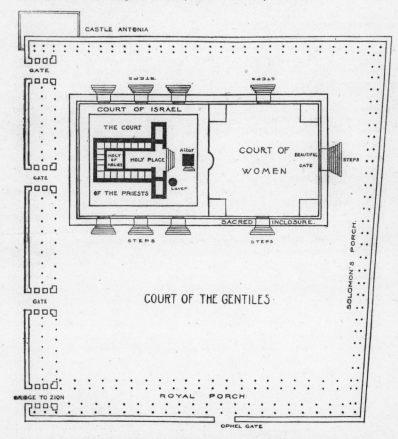

PLAN OF HEROD'S TEMPLE.

LESSON XXV. THE SYNAGOGUE

I. **The Significance of the Word.**—The word "synagogue" comes from the Greek *sunagein: sun,* with + *agein,* to lead. Hence the word "synagogue" means a "*leading together,*" or a "*coming together.*" The Jews were led together because of the common interest they had in the religion of the one true God. It is interesting to compare the words *synagogue* and *church.* "Church" comes from the Greek word meaning "called out," with the idea of "from the world" understood.

II. **An Outgrowth of Necessity.**—Most probably the synagogue arose during the Babylonian captivity, when the temple was in ruins. In this captivity the Jews gathered together in groups for worship and fellowship. We may safely associate the beginning of the synagogue with Ezra.*

III. **Importance of the Synagogue in Biblical History.**

1. **It Kept the Jews from Relapsing into Idolatry.**—It is hardly possible to overestimate the influence of the system thus developed. To it we may ascribe the tenacity with which, after the Maccabean struggle, the Jews adhered to the religion of their fathers, and never again relapsed into idolatry (*Hackett's "Smith's Dictionary of the Bible"*).

2. **A Bible School.**—It was a Bible school, for in it the Scriptures were read and expounded, and thus the study of the Old Testament was promoted.

3. **A House of Worship.**—It was a house of worship and thus perpetuated the worship of the one true and living God.

4. **A Day School.**—It was a schoolhouse for the children during the week, and thus it became an educational center.

5. **Helped Prepare for Christ's Coming.**—As the synagogue spread to many communities, it furnished a place where the gospel might be preached and a people to whom to preach it. The first preachers of the gospel made large use of the synagogue in spreading the new faith.

IV. **How Its Services Were Conducted.**—There were at least three classes of officers in the synagogue:

1. **The Rulers of the Synagogue.**—The chief authorities of the synagogue were a council of elders (also called *rulers* and *shepherds*), of whom one acted as head (the ruler of the synagogue), though only the first among equals. They pronounced excommunications, delivered sentences on offenders of various kinds, managed the charities of the congregation, and attended to the wants of strangers (*Butler*).

2. **Minister** (the hazzan).—An attendant, whose duty was: (1) To unrobe the priests of their vestments. (2) Blow the trumpet for public announcements. (3) Hand the roll of the law to the reader. (4) Act as messenger to the rulers. (5) Inflict scourging.

---

*Dr. W. Dacher, in an exhaustive discussion of the Synagogue, says, "We may confidently place the origin of the Synagogue in Palestine in the period of the Persian domination."

(6) Take charge of the furniture, light the Sabbath lamp and clean the synagogue (*Dowling*).

3. **Batlanim.**—"Ten men of leisure" (*Smith*) who were not obliged to work for their livelihood, and who could attend to the services during the week as well as on the Sabbath. "They were the provincial council, ministering both ecclesiastical and civil affairs" (*Dowling*). They sometimes received a small fee.

BLACKBOARD WORK.

I. The Sig. of the Wo.	II. An Out. of Nec.
III. Its Importance	1. It Ke. the Je. fr. Rel. into Idol. 2. A Bi. Sc. 3. A Ho. of Wor. 4. A Day Sch. 5. Help. Pre. for Chr.'s Com.
IV. How Its Services Were Conducted	1. Rul. of Syn. 2. Min. 3. Batlanim.

TEST QUESTIONS.

1. What does the word "synagogue" mean?
2. During what captivity did it begin?
3. With what person do we associate its origin?
4. How did the synagogue promote the study of the Old Testament?
5. How did the synagogue promote general education?
6. Name two ways that the synagogue aided in preparing the world for Christ.
7. What were the functions of the minister?
8. Who were the "men of ease"?

LESSON XXVI. JEWISH FEASTS

As the Jewish feasts were a part of the worship of God's chosen people, the discussion of them would naturally come in connection with our study of the Jewish institutions of worship. In this lesson we aim to do little more than classify the sacred feasts. By means of a chart outline, we have aimed to bring before the eye the whole matter in concise form.

I. **The Three Great Feasts.**—There were three great feasts known as the Passover, Pentecost and Tabernacles. Pentecost is also spoken of as the feast of the "Weeks," feast of the "Wheat Harvest," and feast of the "Firstfruits." The feast of the Tabernacles is often referred to as the feast of the "Ingathering."

On the occasion of each of these great feasts, every male Israelite was commanded to "appear before the Lord" and make his offering (Deut. 27: 7; Neh. 8: 9-12). "The times of the festivals," says Dr. Smith in his "Dictionary of the Bible," "were evidently ordained in wisdom, so as to interfere as little as possible with the industry of the people. The *Passover* was held just before the work of harvest commenced; *Pentecost* at the conclusion of the corn harvest, and before the vintage; the Feast of *Tabernacles* after all the fruits of the ground were gathered in. In winter, when traveling was difficult, there were no festivals."

CHART OF THE FEASTS OF THE JEWS.

NAME.	DESIGNATION.	MONTH IN WHICH OBSERVED.	NO. OF MONTH OF THE SACRED YEAR.	NO. OF MONTH OF THE CIVIL YEAR.	ENGLISH MONTH NEARLY.	DURATION OF FEAST.	WHERE OBSERVED.	MAIN FEATURE OF ITS OBSERVANCE.	WHAT IT COMMEMORATED.	ALSO CALLED
Passover.	One of the Greater Feasts.	Nisan or Abib.	I.	7	April.	One Week.	Jerusalem.	Eating paschal lamb was chief ceremony.	Passing over of death angel and departure from Egypt.	
Pentecost.	Greater Feast.	Sivan.	III.	9	June.	One Day.	Jerusalem.	Offering two loaves, representing first-fruits of harvest.	Giving the law at Mt. Sinai.	"Weeks," "First-fruits," "Wheat-harvest."
Tabernacles.	Greater Feast.	Tisri or Ethanim.	VII.	1	October.	One Week.	Jerusalem.	Dwelling in booths.	Life in the Wilderness.	"Ingathering."
Purim.	Lesser Feast.	Adar.	XII.	6	March.	Two Days.	Anywhere.	Reading Book of Esther.	Queen Esther's deliverance of Jews from Haman's plot.	
Trumpets.	Lesser Feast.	Ethanim or Tisri.	VII.	1	October.	One Day.	Throughout the land.	Blowing of trumpets.	New Year's Day.	"New Moon."
Dedication.	Lesser Feast.	Chisleu.	IX.	8	December.	Eight Days.	Anywhere.	Great rejoicing, much singing, general illuminating of Jerusalem.	Purging of temple, rebuilding the altar by Judas Maccabeus.	"Lights."

II. The Three Lesser Feasts.—The three lesser feasts were Trumpets, Dedication and Purim. The feast of the Trumpets is often spoken of as the feast of the New Moon. "The feast of Dedication was an annual festival instituted by Judas Maccabæus in 165 B. C. to celebrate the reconsecration of the temple to Jehovah after it had been desecrated for three years by the Greek idolatries carried on within its precincts by order of Antiochus Epiphanes—1 Mac. 4: 52-59 (*Davis' "Dictionary of the Bible"*). Purim was a feast instituted in remembrance of the deliverance of the Jews by Queen Esther from the massacre planned by Haman.

III. The Day of Atonement.—The Day of Atonement was a special fast day for the Hebrews. This was on the tenth day of Ethanim. On this day, the high priest, dressed in white linen, entered the Holy of Holies and sprinkled the blood of the sacrifice upon the mercy-seat of the Ark of the Covenant.

BLACKBOARD WORK.

In the outline on page 60 we have given the (1) name, (2) designation, (3) the Jewish month in which the feast was observed, (4) the number of this month in the sacred year, (5) the number of this month in the civil year, (6) the approximate English month, (7) the duration of the feast, (8) where the feast was observed, (9) the main feature in the observance of the feast, (10) what this feast commemorated, (11) some other names for the feast.

TEST QUESTIONS.

1. Name the three great feasts of the Jews. How were they observed?
2. State what each of the great feasts commemorated.
3. Name the three lesser feasts of the Jews. How were they observed?
4. State what each lesser feast commemorated.
5. What was the only fast-day required by the Jewish law?
6. What special thing was done on this day?

LESSON XXVII. REVIEW OF OLD TESTAMENT INSTITUTIONS

For your review use the "Drill Questions" in the back of this book, from Question 186 to Question 212, inclusive.

PART VII.

SEVEN LESSONS ON THE BIBLE SCHOOL

LESSON XXVIII.   HISTORY OF THE BIBLE SCHOOL

I. As the Bible school is a place to teach the will of God, it will be in place to recall how the teaching of God's will has been an important part of the religious life in all three Bible dispensations. Note:

1. **Abraham** as a teacher (Gen. 18: 19).

2. **Moses** as a teacher (Deut. 4: 9; 11: 19).

3. **Christ** as a teacher. Christ not only was the master Teacher, but he often exhorted his disciples to teach (Matt. 5: 19; 28: 19, 20). Christ, in his training of the twelve, gives us a picture of a wonderful school and a wonderful teacher.

II. **The Modern Bible School.**

1. Robert Raikes, of Gloucester, England, "put the Sunday-school upon the market" in 1780. In 1783 he advocated the establishing of Sunday-schools everywhere.

2. In 1785, in London, the "Society for Promoting Sunday-schools" was organized.

3. At first the Sunday-school had paid teachers, but voluntary teachers were soon introduced. The instruction at first was largely limited to lessons in reading. Afterwards it included the memorizing of Bible verses. Gradually the plans and methods expanded until a systematic study of limited lessons was taken up from week to week, with a loose classification of scholars according to age and attainment. This was the beginning of the well-graded, well-equipped school of to-day.

4. Recognizing the potency of this new Sunday-school agency, John Wesley incorporated it into the policy of his great task. In a letter to his brother Charles, John Wesley said, "The Sunday-school

is one of the noblest institutions which has been set up in Europe for some centuries, and will increase more and more, provided teachers and inspectors do their duty."

5. In 1787 there were 250,000 Sunday-school scholars in Great Britain.

6. The London Sunday-school Union was organized in 1803.

7. The American Sunday-school Union was organized in 1824.

8. The first national convention was held in New York in 1832.

9. The first world's convention was held in London in 1889.

10. The first international convention was held in Baltimore in 1875.

11. The eleventh international convention was held in Toronto, Canada, in 1905.

12. The international lesson system was formally inaugurated early in 1873.

13. The Religious Educational Association was organized in Chicago in 1903.

14. The first Primary Union was organized in the home of Mr. and Mrs. S. W. Clark, Newark, N. J., in 1870. Mrs. S. W. Clark was for ten years its president and instructor. Early in 1871 the New York Union was formed and presided over by Mrs. W. F. Crafts. As a result of her work, the National Primary Union was organized in 1884.

15. The records of teacher-training classes go back as far as 1862, but organized teacher-training work began in 1890, in connection with the Illinois Sunday-school Association. In 1903 the International Sunday-school Association appointed a Committee on Education, and elected a teacher-training superintendent. In 1907 the report showed that fifty-five State and Provincial Associations had approved teacher-training departments.

16. In 1907, when the teacher-training work was well under way, Mr. W. C. Pearce, who had, since 1903, been International Teacher-training Superintendent, was urged to take the position of superintendent of adult work of the International Sunday-school Association. This marked the beginning of the general movement of organized work in the adult department of the Sunday-school.

III. Some Results of the Organized Bible-school Work.

1. The Bible-school army now numbers 29,200,000, distributed as follows: In United States, 14,000,000; in Canada, 1,200,000; in the rest of the world, 14,000,000.

2. In North America alone fully 15,000 conventions are held annually.

3. The Bible school presents the normal evangelism. Not only do 85 per cent. of the Christians come to Christ through the Bible school, but that 85 per cent. forms more than 85 per cent. of the substantial working force of the church.

4. The organized work has produced a very valuable library of religious books. The Bible school is creating a demand for more of them each year.

5. The multitude of suggestive and scholarly lesson helps published by various religious bodies is made possible by the organized Bible-school work.

6. The Bible school has created a wonderful demand for the Bible. In one hundred years the British and Foreign Bible Societies issued more than 180,000,000 copies (complete or in parts) in 370 different languages and dialects. The British Society alone issues 2,000 copies every working hour, or nearly six million annually.

7. The organized work stands for better teaching, better management, better buildings, better equipment, better homes, better communities, and "the whole wide world for Christ."

BLACKBOARD WORK.

MODERN BIBLE SCHOOL.	SOME RESULTS.
1. Robert Raikes.	1. 29,200,000.
2. Paid teachers.	2. 15,000 conventions.
3. John Wesley.	3. Normal evangelism.
4. International lessons.	4. Library.
5. First primary union.	5. Lesson helps.
6. Teacher-training.	6. Bible.
7. Adult work.	7. Better—

TEST QUESTIONS.

1. What has had an important part in the religious life in all three Bible dispensations?
2. Who put the modern Sunday-school on the market?
3. When was the international lesson system inaugurated?
4. When was the first primary union organized?
5. When did organized teacher-training work begin?
6. How many people approximately are there in the Bible-school army?
7. How many conventions are held annually in North America?
8. Name five results of the "Organized Sunday-school Work."

LESSON XXIX. THE BIBLE SCHOOL DEFINED

That the Bible school may do its best work, it must be well understood. Is it the kindergarten of the church? Is it the nursery of the church? Is it a place for children? Yes, the Bible school is all of these, and a great deal more. Men will not come to the Bible school in large numbers if they have the conception that the school is simply a nursery, or a kindergarten. It is therefore necessary to define, rightly and often, the Bible school till the community catches its meaning.

I. The Bible school is the teaching service of the church, to win souls to Christ, and to train them in Christian service.*

1. It is a place for teaching.
2. It is a service of the church.
3. It is to win souls to Christ.

---

*The term "Bible school" is here used because it is being received with favor by many of our leading Bible-school workers of all churches, and because it is a term that honors the Bible, the common text-book in all of our schools. This term appears in the titles of several of the best books, such as Haslett's "Pedagogical Bible School," Pease's "An Outline of a Bible-school Curriculum," and McKinney's "Bible-school Pedagogy." Those, however, who prefer the term "Sunday-school" should substitute it in the definition given above.

4. It is to **train** them in Christian service.

NOTE.—Have your scholars commit this definition to memory. Ask them often to repeat it in concert.

II. Accepting the above definition of the Bible school, several **things** follow:

1. As the Bible school is a church service, every Christian ought to be in it.

2. As the Bible school is a church service, the minister, who stands at the head of the church, should be a leader in this work.

3. As the Bible school is the teaching service of the church, it should have a building well arranged and well equipped for teaching.

4. As the Bible school is the teaching service of the church, it should have thoroughly trained teachers.

5. As one purpose of the Bible school is to win souls to Christ, it should be so organized as to lead the children at the proper time to a personal confession of Christ.

6. As another purpose of the Bible school is to train in Christian service, it should be so organized as to develop a full, round Christian character.

BLACKBOARD WORK.

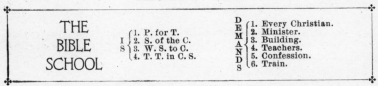

THE BIBLE SCHOOL

IS
1. P. for T.
2. S. of the C.
3. W. S. to C.
4. T. T. in C. S.

DEMANDS
1. Every Christian.
2. Minister.
3. Building.
4. Teachers.
5. Confession.
6. Train.

TEST QUESTIONS.

1. Why should the Bible school not be defined as a "nursery" of the church?
2. What is the objection to calling it the "kindergarten" of the church?
3. Define the Bible school.
4. Who ought to be in the Bible school?
5. What should the minister's part be?
6. What kind of teachers should the "teaching service of the church" have? How can we get them?

LESSON XXX. THE BIBLE SCHOOL AND THE CHURCH

The Bible school lays the foundation upon which all the organizations within the working church build. A Bible-studying church is a **giving, living, growing** and a **go-ing** church. We will consider in this chapter some of the mutual needs of the Bible school and the church as a whole.

I. **Four reasons why the church needs the Bible school:**

1. It needs a **department of education.** To have strong Christians we must instruct the child, the youth and the adult in the facts and doctrines of the Bible.

2. It needs a **workshop.** There is no other department of the church where every one, old or young, can so effectively be kept at work.

3. The church needs a place to **develop Bible teachers.** This is being supplied now in a most satisfactory way through the Bible school.

4. It needs an **evangelizing agency.** Whatever may be said of other methods of evangelizing, the Bible school seems to present the normal way. It takes the child at birth, and instructs and develops him as he grows from period to period, from infancy to adult life.

II. **Four reasons why the Bible school needs the church:**

1. It needs the **hearty co-operation** of all the **officials** of the church. If the Bible school is the teaching service of the church, it needs the leaders of the church to assist in directing its activity.

2. It needs the loyal support of **all members** of the church. Where the Bible school and the church are composed of almost entirely different people, the best work can not be done. In the ideal Bible school, every member of the church is in the school. Those who can not attend its regular meetings on Sunday can belong to the Home Department.

3. It needs the church into which to **lead its members.** A live Bible school will soon win souls to Christ. Those thus won to him should have a local organization in which to work. It is generally true that wherever the Bible school precedes the church in any locality, it soon creates a demand for it.

4. It needs the church to **broaden its interests.** The members of the Bible school should be led to participate heartily in the prayer-meetings, the preaching services, the Lord's Supper, and all normal activities of the church life.

BLACKBOARD WORK.

CHURCH	NEEDS {	1. Dept. of Ed. 2. Workshop. 3. Dev. B. S. Teach. 4. Evang. Agen.
BIBLE SCHOOL	NEEDS {	1. Co-op. of Off. Bd. 2. All Mem. 3. Place into which to lead. 4. Broaden interests.

TEST QUESTIONS.

1. What is the relation of the Bible school to the other organizations within the church?

2. Name four reasons why the church needs the Bible school.

3. Name four reasons why the Bible school needs the church.

4. Name some ways through which the Bible school can keep everybody at work.

5. Why do we say that the Bible school presents the "normal evangelism"?

6. Why should Bible-school workers participate in all other normal activities of the church life?

LESSON XXXI. THE HOME DEPARTMENT

I. **Definition.**—The Home Department is a regular department of the Bible school for those who can not attend the weekly meetings of the school. This department includes physicians, policemen, soldiers, sailors, street-car men, railroad men, liverymen, messenger boys, restaurant waiters, hack drivers, hotel employes, drug clerks, nurses, firemen, many mothers, the aged, those too far away from Bible school, and many others.

II. **Conditions of Belonging to the Home Department.**—There is only one condition. Each member who belongs must promise to study the regular Bible-school lesson at least one-half hour each week. This all Christians and thousands of others will do.

III. **How to Begin.**—Get the approval of your superintendent and minister and then start out. It will help also to have the teachers and officers of the Bible school take favorable action. At first, ask the ones who will be almost certain to join, and then, with their influence and encouragement, go on with enthusiasm. If any hesitate, tell them that

(1) The work requires less than five minutes' study each day.

(2) There are no dues or fees to pay. The offerings are entirely voluntary and amply cover expenses.

(3) If any one does not like it, he can stop at any time.

IV. **How Many It Takes.**—Having secured one person, you have a Home Department. Repeat this work indefinitely until you have covered your field.

V. **Its Benefits.**

1. Through the Home Department, thousands are regularly studying the Bible who otherwise would not.

2. It restores in many homes the much-needed family altar.

3. It makes many indifferent Christians "different." Their inactivity is displaced by activity.

4. It increases the attendance at the regular sessions of the school.

5. It makes it possible to enroll the whole church in the Bible school.

6. It develops Christian workers.

7. It more than pays for itself financially, as well as socially, mentally and spiritually.

VI. **Visitors.**—Each Home Department superintendent should select enough visitors to help him in the work. These visitors canvass the field to secure members. They also call at the end of the quarter to deliver the new quarterlies and record envelopes and receive the report and the offering for the three months just passed. Each visitor can probably look after about ten members. The visitors make a quarterly report to the Home Department superintendent, who makes a quarterly report before the whole school. Many ministers are their own Home Department superintendents, and we find that in their hands the work is a wonderful success.

VII. **Some Things to Do.**

1. Get the minister to preach on the subject.

2. Have the Bible-school superintendent announce it from the platform.

3. Make a house-to-house visitation of everybody in the community.

4. Have a preview of the lessons of the quarter presented by the minister on Sunday evening or at some other suitable time.

5. Have regular meetings with your visitors.

6. Organize messenger and sunshine bands.

7. Keep tactfully and unreservedly at it.

BLACKBOARD WORK.

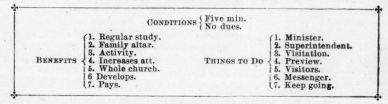

CONDITIONS { Five min. / No dues.

BENEFITS {
1. Regular study.
2. Family altar.
3. Activity.
4. Increases att.
5. Whole church.
6 Develops.
7. Pays.

THINGS TO DO {
1. Minister.
2. Superintendent.
3. Visitation.
4. Preview.
5. Visitors.
6. Messenger.
7. Keep going.

TEST QUESTIONS.

1. Who should constitute the Home Department?

2. What is the one condition of belonging to the Home Department?

3. Name seven benefits of such a department.

4. Name seven things to do to make it a success.

5. Name the steps you would take in organizing a Home Department.

LESSON XXXII. GRADING THE SCHOOL

I. **The Need of the Graded School.**

1. The great need of most Bible schools is better system about their work. Many schools could be doubled in thoroughness and numbers by being thoroughly organized. Organization distributes responsibility, develops workers, and secures promptness and thoroughness.

2. All schools that have more than one class are more or less graded. In every school there is a kind of assorting of pupils into groups, with reference to age and attainment. This is the beginning of grading. Since every school is in a sense graded, our discussion must deal with the problem of how to grade a school thoroughly.

3. That we may feel more keenly the need of a carefully organized and graded school, we ask each reader to answer these questions: Can you place your finger on certain things to be learned in a given time because it is specifically planned that these be taught at that time? Have you any specific thing laid down to be accomplished by your school by December 31? Do you have a time and place for teaching the books of the Bible, Bible geography, outlines of Old Testament history, and of the lives of Christ and Paul? Do you give your scholars a promotion as an incentive to study? Does the community in which you live look upon the work of your

school as superficial? Do you use any slipshod methods? Do you know how to win people to Christ? Are the ideals of your school high? Is there an unwritten law that a teacher, whether good or not, may, like Tennyson's brook, run on forever? Is tardiness looked upon as a disgrace? Is your school a school in reality or only in name? Do you have a systematic way of enrolling new pupils? Do you have a good follow-up system? Are your teachers becoming specialists in their various departments? The rightly "graded school" will rightly answer these and many other questions.

4. The graded Bible school is one that fits the Bible to the scholar as he develops from year to year and from period to period.

II. **Seven Essentials of a Graded School.**

1. **Departments and Grades.**—The departments are **Cradle Roll, Beginners', Primary, Junior, Intermediate, Adult and Home.** Many schools divide those over sixteen years of age into two departments —the senior department and the adult department. By grades is meant the division within the departments. For example, in the primary department proper, there are three grades—those who will be seven, those who will be eight, and those who will be nine by promotion day. These grades correspond in a general way to the first, second and third grades in the public school. The highest grade in each department is called the graduating class. So each school can have a primary graduating class, a junior graduating class, an intermediate graduating class, and so on.

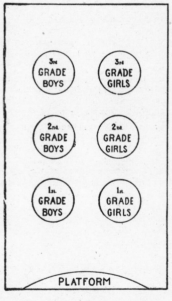

This diagram shows the arrangement of a junior department, with three grades and six classes. The same plan of grading may be followed in the primary department proper. This general plan may be followed even where the department does not have a separate room. Once a year each class is promoted. The first grade is promoted to the second, the second to the third, and the third grade is graduated to the next department. The third grade is known as the graduation class, and is so designated for the entire year.

2. **Departments Organized.**—Each department has a superintendent or principal, a secretary, and enough teachers to take care of the scholars of that department. Some schools also have an assistant department superintendent, a secretary, an organist, etc. The general superintendent's work in such a school becomes more difficult, but also more effective. He is the chief executive.

3. **Enrollment Secretary.**—The work of the enrollment secre-

tary is to receive each new scholar and place him in his proper department and grade. Here is an enrollment secretary's card, which will explain itself:

```
Name ........................................................................
No. and St. ......................... ....................... Date of Birth ...............
School Grade. ..........................Church Membership..................
Date Enrolled...........................School Formerly Attended ...........
Assigned to Grade or Class ...................Department................
Graduated to ....................................Dept. Date...........
Graduated to ....................................Dept. Date.......... ......
Graduated to ....................................Dept. Date...........
Father's Name .................................. Father's Church...............
Mother's Name ................................ Mother's Church...............

Date Dropped..................... Cause...... ......... .................
```

The enrollment secretary has general charge of the grading, and sees that the school keeps graded.

4. **Adaptation of Teachers.**—In every successful school, the teachers are fitted to their scholars. By that we mean that those who can teach children best are assigned to teach them; those who can teach adults best are enlisted in the adult work.

5. **Adaptation of Lessons.**—Each lesson should be taught to fit the scholar. Hence the presentation of lessons to the primary children will be different from that which would be suitable for a class of young men. When a teacher becomes efficient in any department he ought not to leave that department. He should go with his class through the grades of that department, and then, when his class graduates, he should take another from a lower department and teach it as it passes through the department in which he has become a specialist. This will put a class under the same teacher for three or four years, according to the department. In the adult department the teachers remain with their classes indefinitely.

6. **Supplemental Lessons.**—This is one of the most important, if not the most important, of the seven features of the graded school. This work is fundamental. Through supplemental lessons many things can be taught that otherwise must be left untouched. Graded supplemental lessons make the scholars feel that they are growing as year by year they meet the requirements and receive their certificates, diplomas and seals.*

7. **Regular Promotion Day.**—When the scholars are doing a certain definite work each month throughout the year, there should be one day when this work is recognized and when all the scholars under sixteen years of age will pass up one grade. If they have satisfactorily completed the supplemental lessons, they are given certificates, diplomas or seals, according to the department and grade. If they do not satisfactorily complete the work, they are passed on without such recognition. If they do especially good work,

---

*For a full discussion of supplemental work and a suggestion as to "how to begin to grade," see Lesson XXXIII.

"With Honor" is written upon their certificates, diplomas or seals. Regular promotion and graduation day is a time of great importance in all schools that observe it. Through it, the school may make its impression upon the community as it can in no other way. This annual promotion day may be at any time, but it is suggested that it either be in January or in June.

III. **Benefits of a Graded School.**

1. Makes knowledge appetizing.
2. Makes teaching definite.
3. Raises the standard of teaching.
4. Gives workable knowledge of the Bible.
5. Utilizes the value of promotions and graduations.
6. Gives an impression of thoroughness. It impresses not only the members of the school, but the community, as being Biblical, pedagogical, reasonable, inspirational, and workable.

BLACKBOARD WORK.

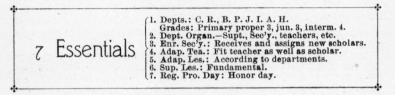

7 Essentials

1. Depts.: C. R., B. P. J. I. A. H.
   Grades: Primary proper 3, jun. 3, interm. 4.
2. Dept. Organ.—Supt., Sec'y., teachers, etc.
3. Enr. Sec'y.: Receives and assigns new scholars.
4. Adap. Tea.: Fit teacher as well as scholar.
5. Adap. Les.: According to departments.
6. Sup. Les.: Fundamental.
7. Reg. Pro. Day: Honor day.

TEST QUESTIONS.

1. Name the great needs of the Bible school.
2. Define the graded school.
3. Name the seven essentials of a graded school.
4. Name the departments of a well-organized school.
5. How long should a baby be kept on the Cradle Roll?
6. At what age are the Beginners promoted to the primary department proper?
7. At what age are the primary children promoted to the junior department?
8. When are the juniors to be promoted? The intermediates?
9. What are some of the benefits of the graded school?

LESSON XXXII'. GRADED SUPPLEMENTAL LESSONS

I. **The Purpose.**—Supplemental lessons are in no sense a substitute for the International or any other series of lessons, but are intended to render these systems more complete and effective.

II. **The Necessity.**—We must face the fact that many of our Bible schools are not giving the scholars a systematic and connected knowledge of the Bible. The censure for this is not to be placed at the door of the International system of lessons, nor of any other system. All such systems must be modified, as even a cursory effort in the preparation of a course of study will show. Some extra work must be brought into our schools:

1. That will fit memory passages to each grade.

2. That will familiarize the scholars with the books of the Bible, and keywords as to the contents of the same.

3. That will blaze the way through the Old and New Testament history as outline work into which each Sunday's lesson may be fitted.

4. That will teach the best church hymns.

5. That will teach Bible geography.

6. That will serve, in the main, as a basis of promotions and graduations.

III. All Agree.—The value of a systematic and connected knowledge of the word of God is not questioned by any. Bible study possesses a new charm when such work is well done. Teachers can not only teach better, but they can teach more, and with greater ease. When the objection is raised that there is not time enough in the regular period allotted to the Bible school to do supplemental work, we answer that such work in the long run saves time, and, furthermore, increases our knowledge of and intensifies our interest in Bible study.

IV. The Plan.—In a course of supplemental lessons, the writer should indicate approximately the proper amount of work that should be attempted each month. This, of course, may be modified. Where the Scripture is given for the entire year without being divided into months, there is a tendency to leave the work until the end is approaching and then rush for the examination.

V. How to Begin.—From the chart on page 83 you will readily see the plan that is followed in many of our best graded schools. To bring any school into the thoroughly graded work can not be done in a night. Do not attempt it. It is best to begin by grading those below twelve years of age. This includes the Beginners' class, the three grades in the primary and three grades in the junior departments. Then group all those above twelve in their approximate departments. Suppose, for instance, you have in your school four classes, the majority of whom are between the ages of twelve and sixteen. Call those classes your intermediate department. It is not best to take scholars above twelve out of their classes and make the grades at first. This will come about gradually and naturally. Then, for your senior department, group all those from sixteen up. Each scholar in the school should have a supplemental booklet suited to his department and grade. The first year it will be better for all over twelve to use the same booklet.

VI. The Time.—In most of the primary departments from ten to twenty minutes are given to the supplemental lesson; in the departments above the primary, from five to ten minutes. A part of this time, at least, is taken from the opening and closing exercises rather than from the regular lesson recitation period. The superintendent or the minister should have a two-minute drill frequently, calling forth the work that is being done. It should also be woven into the regular exercises.

VII. The Small School.—There are many schools that are not large enough to have a separate class in each one of the grades.

There are schools where the primary department does not enroll more than twelve scholars, and these are taught by one teacher. The question then presents itself, "How can I teach three different grades of work to the whole class?" The problem is easily solved. Suppose that of these twelve children, four of them will be seven by the next promotion day, four of them eight by promotion day, and four of them nine by promotion day. Call those that will be nine your primary graduates. Select two helpers. Girls of fifteen and sixteen are often very excellent in this work. Get one of your helpers to teach the supplemental work to the first grade, the other to the second grade, then you teach the third grade. You will also teach the uniform lesson to the entire twelve and to the two helpers.

VIII. **Any School Can Use These Lessons.**—In all schools, the supplemental lessons can be used, whether graded or ungraded. The best results, however, will be attained in graded schools, where the supplemental lessons, together with age, form the basis of promotions and graduations. Many of the schools that have not been using supplemental work may start with some easy work and drill the entire school upon that.

IX. **Difficulties.**—Some difficulties will probably present themselves, and wisdom and patience must always be shown. Do not try to do this work all at once. No great work is accomplished in a day. Set your ideal and then work toward it. Gradually readjust your present classes, and in the meantime the new scholars will have been assigned to their proper departments and grades. In the beginning, do not attempt too much. Proceed carefully, but determine in time to make your school one of the very best.

NOTE.—Before taking up this lesson, the teacher should write to various publishing-houses and get samples of supplemental booklets to show to the class.

BLACKBOARD WORK.

Supplemental Lessons Should Cover	1. Memory passages fitted to each grade. 2. The books of the Bible and their divisions. 3. Outlines of Old and New Testament history. 4. The best church hymns. 5. Outlines of Bible geography.

Supplemental lessons serve, in the main, as a basis of promotions and graduations.

NOTE.—For further blackboard work use chart on page 74 and the diagram on page 69.

TEST QUESTIONS.

1. What is the purpose of supplemental lessons?
2. Through supplemental work name four things that should be taught.
3. Answer the objection that there is not time enough to teach supplemental lessons.
4. How would you begin to grade a school and introduce graded supplemental work?
5. How do supplemental lessons aid in grading a school?

LESSON XXXIV. REVIEW OF THE BIBLE SCHOOL

Turn to the "Drill Questions" and use Questions 213 to 224, inclusive. Review also the first 212 questions.

PRIMARY.			JUNIOR.		INTERMEDIATE.		SENIOR OR ADULT.			
0–3	3–6	6–9	9 — 12		12 — 16					
CRADLE ROLL.	BEGIN-NERS.	Primary Proper.	First Second Third Grade Grade Grade		First Second Third Fourth Grade Grade Grade Grade		TEACHER TRAINING.	CHRISTIAN TRAINING.	MISSION TRAINING.	ADVANCED COURSES.
		First Second Third Grade Grade Grade								

HOME DEPARTMENT.

Cradle Roll; birth to three. (CRADLE ROLL PROPORTION CERTIFICATE.)

Beginners, three to six. (BEGINNERS' PROPORTION CERTIFICATE.)

For those who will be Seven by Promotion Day. (CERTIFICATE.)

For those who will be Eight by Promotion Day. (CERTIFICATE.)

For those who will be Nine by Promotion Day. PRIMARY DIPLOMA.

For those who will be Ten by Promotion Day. (YELLOW SEAL OR CERTIFICATE.)

For those who will be Eleven by Promotion Day. (ORANGE SEAL OR CERTIFICATE.)

For those who will be Twelve by Promotion Day. JUNIOR DIPLOMA.

For those who will be Thirteen by Promotion Day. (BLUE SEAL OR CERTIFICATE.)

For those who will be Fourteen by Promotion Day. (PINK SEAL OR CERTIFICATE.)

For those who will be Fifteen by Promotion Day. (GREEN SEAL OR CERTIFICATE.)

For those who will be Sixteen by Promotion Day. (INTERMEDIATE) DIPLOMA.

For young people over sixteen, the same supplementary work for the entire department.

Certificates are given on Promotion Day.

For Adults, supplemental work optional.

The above chart will bring before you an outline of the best graded Bible schools. It may be adapted to any school, whether large or small. We know both from experience and observation that such a grading is possible, practical, pedagogical, and potent. The double lines show the division of the departments, and the single lines the grades within the department. While the Cradle Roll and the Beginners' departments are distinct from the primary department, still in most cases they should be under the general charge of the primary superintendent.

From grade to grade in the junior and intermediate departments you will note that it reads "Seal or certificate." Those who have diplomas receive seals, but those who have no diplomas would have nothing on which to place the seals, so they are given certificates.

The line of ? marks indicates that there may be a division of the younger folks and the older ones in the senior or adult department, but that there is no definite age for the transfer. As the International Adult Department includes all persons over sixteen years of age, it is likely that the Bible schools generally will also accept the name "adult" for that department in the local schools. The adult department may be subdivided to suit the individual school. In the above chart, it might be well to leave out the word SENIOR and let the word ADULT include all persons sixteen years of age and upward.

All certificates, diplomas, and seals mentioned in this chart may be secured from the publishers of this book.

PART VIII.

EIGHT LESSONS ON THE TEACHER AND HIS WORK

LESSON XXXV. THE TEACHER'S QUALIFICATIONS

I. **The Secret of a Successful School.**—Let me ask you to face squarely for a moment this question: "What makes a successful Bible school?" There is but one answer, **"The Teacher."**

In her **Talks with the Training Class,** Margaret Slattery says: "Lesson courses broad in conception and rich in material, fitted to the needs of the various pupils, are absolutely necessary, but they can not make a successful school. Rooms adapted to Sunday-school needs, music, maps, the stereopticon, wisely chosen pictures and libraries, all the machinery of an up-to-date Sunday-school—these are most necessary in solving the problem, but these can not make a successful school; no system of grading, however carefully planned and carried out, no examination questions, promotion exercises or diplomas, not even large numbers in attendance, can make a successful school if the teacher, the right sort of a teacher, be lacking. A teacher of the right sort will make use of as many of these means as possible, but he and not they will make the school a success."

II. **An Acrostic.**—The right sort of a teacher must have several qualifications, which, for memory's sake, we discuss through the means of an acrostic. He must be:

Trained.
Enthusiastic.
Ambitious.
Conscientious.
Happy.
Early.
Real.

1. **Trained.**—The time is already here in many schools when no

one but a trained teacher is permitted to teach. Some one has said that there are two things that many people would undertake to do without preparation—edit a newspaper, and teach in a Bible school. Whatever may be the case concerning the newspaper, the Bible school must come to the place where it will demand of its teachers a thorough knowledge (1) of the Bible, (2) of the scholar, and (3) of the principles and methods of teaching.

2. **Enthusiastic.**—Enthusiasm is a vital part of education. It is as contagious as the measles. If you want to know whether or not you are enthusiastic, simply observe whether the people with whom you associate get enthusiastic on the things in which you are most interested.

3. **Ambitious.**—It is perfectly proper for every teacher and Bible-school worker to try to excel. Make your class the best class, your department the best department, your school the best school. Try to be the best trained teacher in the school. Often the difference between success and failure is the difference between ambition and laziness.

4. **Conscientious.**—To live as Christ would have us live and as we would have our scholars live is an absolute essential of an ideal teacher. Miss Margaret Slattery tells the story of how one day she told Charlie in particular, and the whole school in general, not to run over the lawn that day, as it had been raining and the lawn was soft. After dismissing her scholars in the evening, she hastened to get ready to go out to a dinner party. As she went to the door of the schoolroom, she saw the car coming, and the only car that would get her to the place in time for the dinner. But, to reach that car she would have to run over the lawn that she had told Charlie in particular, and the school in general, not to cross. The tempter said, "Don't be foolish; run right across the lawn, catch your car and meet your engagement. Your scholars will not know it, for they are all gone." Her better self said, "No, you must not. You told the scholars they must not, and you must live out your teaching." The car went off without her, but she was left with a clear conscience and the confidence of her scholars.

5. **Happy.**—The Bible school is one of the happiest places possible. No teacher is qualified to teach unless he has a happy disposition. If our Christianity is real, it will show itself in our every deed and smile and spoken word.

6. **Early.**—This may not seem on a par with the other qualifications mentioned, but it reveals the habit   Lateness to Sunday-school is not caused by late work on Saturday or extra children to dress. It is simply a habit. Marion Lawrance says, "Some teachers have three hands, a right hand, a left hand, and a little behind hand." If this is true of you, amputate the little behind hand immediately. We might write over some of the classroom doors, "*The late John Jones, teacher of Class No. 17.*" The mere fact that we are late and our scholars are early may counteract most of the good we try to do.

7. **Real.**—Each teacher should be a real Christian, and a real friend before his scholars. Do not pretend to be over-religious on

the one hand, nor irreverent on the other. If you are teaching a class of steam-engine boys, be a real boy with the boys. If you are teaching young people, mix into their joys and difficulties a whole-hearted, happy religion.

The ideal teacher's ideal is to be of the largest possible service in developing the lives of his scholars. He must realize that every lesson that he teaches must have an influence directly or indirectly upon the scholars he is teaching. His passion must be a *passion for service*. Our master Teacher "came not to be ministered unto, but to minister, and to give his life a ransom for many" (Matt. 20: 28). Not wealth, not pleasure, not fame, but *service*, is the measure of success.

BLACKBOARD WORK.

For blackboard work use the acrostic on the word T-E-A-C-H-E-R.

TEST QUESTIONS.

1. Why should a teacher be trained for his work?
2. Why is enthusiasm a vital part of education?
3. What part does ambition have in teaching?
4. Can an ideal teacher teach without living what he is teaching?
5. Can a "sour"-dispositioned teacher teach well?
6. Why is promptness a vital part of a teacher's life?
7. Give the acrostic on the teacher.

LESSON XXXVI. THE TEACHER'S PREPARATION

I. **The Teacher's Preparation of Himself.**—For the teacher to master himself is as important as for him to master his subject. Three helps for the teacher's mastery of himself in his preparation for teaching are:

1. **Prayer.**—Prayer is a high privilege. It is a mighty power. It keeps the teacher in tune with the master Teacher. Pray for your scholars every day. Cultivate the habit of thinking earnestly and continuously about their spiritual interests.

2. **Study.**—Not the study of next Sunday's lesson simply, but a systematic study of the whole Bible. Aim to know more than you expect to teach. It is what you do not say that gives force to what you do say.

3. **Conversation.**—Cultivate the habit of talking with the best men and women. Seek the broadest culture possible in the circumstances in which you are placed.

II. **The Teacher's Preparation of His Lesson.**

1. **Three Steps in Lesson Preparation.**—There are three steps in the teacher's preparation of his lesson that should ever be kept in view:

(1) **Facts.**—The first step is to get the facts of the lesson, and all things connected therewith. Do not read into the Bible your own opinions, but humbly let it speak to you and accept its dictations. At this point in your lesson preparation, keep your class as much as possible out of your mind. The primary teacher who picks up her primary quarterly the first

thing in preparing her lesson is going at it from the wrong end.

(2) **Facts for self.**—After you have mastered the facts of the lesson thoroughly, go over it again with the view of applying it to your own life. Under the first step you study the lesson till you get a hold upon it; under this step you study the lesson till it gets a hold upon you.

(3) **Facts for scholars.**—After once you have a firm hold upon the lesson, and after the lesson has a firm hold upon your own spiritual life, you are then ready to study it again with a view to adapting it to the needs of your scholars, both collectively and individually.

2. **Methods in Lesson Preparation.**

(1) **Seven Element Method.**—In every lesson these seven elements may be found.

(a) **Places.**—One or more, named in the text or implied.

(b) **Persons.**—Who they were and what is known of them.

(c) **Dates.**—The year and period in history.

(d) **Doings.**—What the people in the lesson did and said.

(e) **Difficulties.**—Through obscure terms, Oriental customs, and the like.

(f) **Doctrines.**—General religious principles taken directly or indirectly from the lesson.

(g) **Duties.**—Practical lessons enforced by the whole subject considered.

(2) **Angle Method.**—This method is widely used in teachers' meetings, and is very helpful for directing the individual in his study.

Angle No. 1—**Approach.**—Give the subject of last lesson, brief intervening history, and circumstances leading to this lesson. Let the lesson text be read at this point.

Angle No. 2—**The Lesson Story.**—Give briefly in your own words the story of the lesson.

Angle No. 3—**Analysis.**—Give one or more simple outlines to aid in studying and teaching this lesson. Use the blackboard if possible.

Angle No. 4—**Biography.**—Give the names of all persons, classes and nations referred to in the lessons.

Angle No. 5—**Oriental Lights.**—Give any Oriental customs peculiar to the lesson.

Angle No. 6—**Questions.**—Ask two or more questions that will suggest lines of thought.

Angle No. 7—**Leading Thoughts.**—Give one or more leading thoughts, and the reason for your selection.

Angle No. 8—**Approach.**—Give one way of introducing the lesson, that attention may be secured from the start.

Angle No. 9—**Beginners, primary, junior, intermediate, adult.**—Give the features of this lesson which are adapted to your department.

Angle No. 10—**Illustrations.**—Give one or more apt illustrations.

Angle No. 11—Practical Lessons.—Give one or more practical lessons that may naturally be drawn from the facts of the lesson.

III. **The Teacher's Preparation of His Scholars.**—"How can I prepare my scholars to receive the lesson?" some teacher may ask. In many ways, two of which we here note:

1. **By gaining confidence.**—Cultivate such personal relations with each pupil, both on Sunday and during the week, as will inspire confidence in your judgment and personal life.

2. **By assigning work.**—"How can I secure home study?" is an oft-asked question. We answer:

(a) **Assign it.**
(b) **Expect it.**
(c) **Call for it.**
(d) **Commend it.**
(e) **Use it.**

IV. **Hints on Lesson Preparation.**

1. Begin early.
2. Keep the connected sweep of history always in mind.
3. Use the Bible first, and then lesson helps liberally.
4. Write down outlines of the lessons. This is hard at first, but it is an art that can soon be mastered.
5. Think for yourself. Use the thoughts of others, not to displace, but to aid your own thoughts.
6. Go to the teachers' meetings to give and to get.
7. Talk with others about the lessons.

BLACKBOARD WORK.

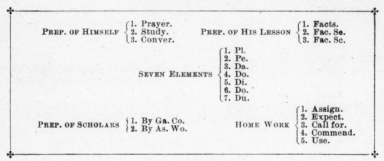

TEST QUESTIONS.

1. Name three elements in the teacher's preparation of himself.
2. Name the three steps in lesson preparation.
3. Name the seven elements found in every lesson.
4. Name two ways to prepare the scholars to receive the lessons.
5. Tell how to secure home study.
6. Give five hints on lesson preparation.

LESSON XXXVII. PRINCIPLES IN TEACHING

1. Principles are the foundations upon which all work is done, and methods are the plans of building in accordance with them.

> "Methods are many, principles are few;
> Methods may vary, principles never do."

2. All human activity must be in accordance with certain definite laws or principles. It goes without saying, therefore, that all true teaching must be done in accordance with the true principles of instruction. Of these principles, we mention six:

I. **Put the New in an Old Setting.**—This is another statement of the old law that we must proceed from the known to the unknown. The teacher must begin where the scholar is, that the scholar may end where the teacher is. The new is to be received and understood by what the scholar has experienced which is similar to it. This principle demands:

1. That the teacher find what the scholar knows, or does not know, about the lesson.

2. That he proceed from the known to the unknown by single, simple, sensible steps. Material should be arranged in a systematic order, so each thought will connect itself with the succeeding thought.

II. **Use Words that are Understood by the Teacher and the Scholar in the Same Sense.** This principle demands:

1. That the teacher know the vocabulary of the class, both collectively and individually.

2. That the teacher be careful to explain any unfamiliar words that he finds necessary to use.

III. **Adapt the Teaching to the Needs of the Scholar.**—To know what truths an individual needs and is able to receive, the teacher must look at him in relation to his inner life and his week-day influences.

1. **Inner Life.**
   (1) Knowledge.
   (2) Temperament.
   (3) Spiritual condition.
2. **Seven Week-day Influences.**
   (1) Home.
   (2) School.
   (3) Street.
   (4) Reading.
   (5) Recreation.
   (6) Companions.
   (7) Occupation.

IV. **Secure Co-operation.**—The teacher must have the co-operation of the scholars. This principle demands:

1. An attention given heartily in response to interest.

2. That the scholars be directed in their search after truth.

3. That the scholars be kept busy every moment. "All the class all the time" is the motto.

4. That the scholars be kept busy during the week, in study and in other work.

V. **The Development of the Subject Must Constantly Present New Points of Interest.**—This is called the "law of sustained interest." This may be done by:

1. Using the scholar's activity, both mental and physical.

2. Placing the old in a new setting. Adults as well as children like to see new combinations made of things familiar to them.

3. Making use of curiosity and suspense.

4. Sustained interest on the part of the teacher.

VI. **Ideas Must be Repeated to be Retained.**—Concerning this principle four points are noted:

1. Things that are to be remembered must be frequently reviewed.

2. Both teacher and scholar enjoy knowing some things well.

3. Have a rapid review every Sunday.

4. Monthly, quarterly, and annual reviews should not be neglected.

TWELVE PRACTICAL POINTS IN TEACHING.

NOTE.—Study these carefully, but it is not necessary to commit them.

1. A story must be pointed to be potent.

2. Use illustrations freely, but not foolishly.

3. Your life must be an illustration of what you teach.

4. We may judge the impressions we give by the expressions we get.

5. Be considerate of what people want to know, and they will be considerate concerning what you want them to know.

6. Every person is a distinct individual. Study him as such.

7. You are teaching a growing individual first, and a subject second.

8. Teach your scholars not only to "be good," but to be good for something.

9. Be accurate in what the scholars know, and they will believe you to be accurate in what they do not know.

10. Understand where you are going when you begin, that your scholars may know where you are when you get through.

11. Keep a good reserve force. It is unsafe to tell all you know.

12. The teacher's **Rule of Three:**
Three things to be—true, thorough, thoughtful.
Three things to govern—time, temper, tongue.
Three things to cherish—love, liberty, life.
Three things to love—honor, home, heaven
Three things to educate—hand, head, heart.
Three things to consider—duty, death, destiny.

BLACKBOARD WORK.

I. NEW IN OLD	{ 1. Test. { 2. Step by step.	II. WORDS UNDERSTOOD	{ 1. Vocab. { 2. Explain.
III. ADAPTED	{ 1. Kno. Tem. Spi. { 2. Seven week-day.	IV. CO-OPERATION	{ 1. Atten. { 2. Direct. { 3. All the class. { 4. During week.
V. NEW POINTS	{ 1. Sc. Act. { 2. Old in Ne. { 3. Cur. Sus. { 4. Int. in Tea.	VI. REPETITION	{ 1. Fre. Re. { 2. Enjoy. { 3. Ev. Su. { 4. Mo. Qu. Ye.

TEST QUESTIONS.

1. What is the difference between principles and methods in teaching?
2. Name six principles in teaching.
3. Name six week-day influences surrounding the scholars.
4. Name four ways of sustaining interest in the development of the lesson.
5. What do you understand by the "vocabulary" of the class?
6. Why are reviews necessary?

LESSON XXXVIII. FIVE FORMAL STEPS IN TEACHING

Our last lesson considered general principles in teaching. Now it will be well to discuss how an actual lesson may be conducted. All successful teachers realize that there is an advantage in adopting some general plan of procedure that may be followed in teaching every lesson. This aids the memory, saves time, economizes energy, and makes teaching more definite and helpful. In the teaching of every lesson there is a part that remains uniform, and a part that varies. The uniform part deals with the form of the lesson rather than the matter, hence we call it the "formal" element. In the process of teaching any lesson this formal part may be divided into a certain number of "formal steps." Of these steps there are five:

I. **Testing.**—All previous knowledge is a preparation for each lesson that we are to teach. In presenting any lesson it is absolutely necessary for the teacher to know where his scholars are relative to their knowledge of the subject to be studied. Testing **consists in finding out which of the ideas in the scholar's mind are in any way connected with the present lesson, and in bringing forth from his storehouse of ideas all that are likely to be of service.** Testing may be a little difficult at first, but the wise teacher very quickly learns what ideas among his pupils he can depend upon.

1. **Not Scrappy.**—The teacher who can successfully test his pupils can not be "scrappy" in his teaching. He must know something more than last Sunday's and next Sunday's lessons. He must see the sweep of history for the entire quarter, and for the entire year. There is a close connection among almost all of the lessons, and this connection is necessary in rightly testing the scholar.

2. **Law of the Mind.**—This formal step is based upon the following law of the mind: "The mind can receive new knowledge only through similar ideas already known."

3. **One Question.**—The one question the teacher asks himself under this heading, is: "What do my scholars know about the subject in hand?"

II. **Presentation.**—"Testing" is **finding the foundation, and "presentation" is building thereon.** Presentation begins where the scholars are, and not of necessity with the present lesson. A boy was being asked a series of related questions which he answered promptly. Finally the teacher asked a question beyond his knowledge, and he replied, "That's just as far as my thinker will go." This is where presentation comes in. Begin where your scholars are, and present the intervening facts that will lead up to the lessons of the day. This will keep your lessons from being "scrappy."

1. **Method.**—The method of presentation will be the story for the primary children, the question method for the juniors and intermediates, and a combination of the question and the lecture methods for the young people and adults.

2. **Two Essentials.**—The presentation of new ideas must be:
   (1) **In the proper order.**—The poor story-teller will sometimes say, "But I forgot to tell you so and so." Such an interpolation is made when the speaker comes to the place where he realizes that a certain fact is lacking. Getting facts out of their order not only causes confusion, but often results in the whole point being lost.
   (2) **Through co-operation.**—Effective teaching can not be done unless the teacher has the hearty co-operation of the scholars.

NOTE.—Under presentation the teacher should give the historic setting, explain the lesson difficulties, and bring out its facts.

III. **Association.**—**The interweaving of the new ideas into the scholar's previously acquired knowledge is called "association."** The new must be associated with the old in order that the latter may be retained.

1. **Two ways association** may be made:
   (1) By grouping similar ideas.
   (2) By gathering together dissimilar ideas and comparing them.

NOTE.—Under this heading Bible illustrations may most helpfully be used.

IV. **Generalization.**—The comparison of ideas, as mentioned under association, naturally leads to this step. Having gathered together much data, the scholar is ready to deduce therefrom a broad statement, which we call **generalization. Generalization is therefore a broad statement of truth, deduced from facts under consideration.** If the association of ideas has been carefully and wisely done, we can not go seriously wrong in generalization.

Illustration.—Suppose we are studying the "Call of Abram." We compare his call, in similarities and differences, with those of Moses and Paul; and then sum it all up in the generalization: **"A man with a great faith will have a great future."** Or, "God's calls lead to surrendered service and sure success."

V. **Application.**—This is a fitting final formal step. One rule in teaching is, "Impression must lead to expression." If all of the impressions made in the first four steps do not lead the scholar to the point where he feels the practical bearing of the truths of the lesson upon his own life, the lesson is a failure. **The application translates the theory into knowledge, the words into works.** It should be brief, pointed, catchy, general in the class, and personal in private.

These are the five "formal steps." They must be faithfully used to be fully understood. To be conscious of a definite plan in teaching every lesson will give the teacher both pleasure and power in his work.

BLACKBOARD WORK.

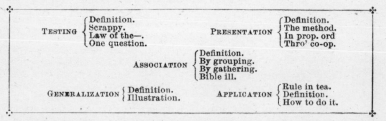

TESTING	Definition. Scrappy. Law of the—. One question.	PRESENTATION	Definition. The method. In prop. ord Thro' co-op.
	ASSOCIATION	Definition. By grouping. By gathering. Bible ill.	
GENERALIZATION	Definition. Illustration.	APPLICATION	Rule in tea. Definition. How to do it.

TEST QUESTIONS.

1. Name the five formal steps in teaching.
2. What do you understand by testing a scholar?
3. What law of the mind is testing based upon?
4. What one question should the teacher ask himself under the first step?
5. What is the difference between testing and presentation?
6. What will be the method of presentation in the primary department? In the junior and intermediate departments? In the adult department?
7. Give two rules in presenting new ideas.
8. Define the step called association.
9. Give two ways association may be made.
10. Define the step called generalization.
11. Name and define the final formal step.
12. How should the application be made?

LESSON XXXIX. A STUDY OF THE MIND

Our aim in this lesson is simply to familiarize the student with the most common terms used in studying the mind. Ruric N. Roark says that a teacher must know three M's, "Matter, Mind and Method." In this series of lessons we have studied much about the first M, we now consider the second.

I. **Attention.**—Attention is "focused consciousness." When consciousness is concentrated upon a single object, we have attention.

James Sully says that attention is "the ability to detain objects before the mind."

The problem of securing attention is a vital one. Without attention there is no teaching. One might as well try to pour oil into a bottle with the cork in, as attempt to teach without attention. Among the methods of securing attention we mention five, each of which begins with C.

1. **Contact.**—The teacher, in introducing a new idea, begins at the point in the scholar's knowledge which is nearest the idea he wishes to present. This is the "point of contact."

2. **Curiosity.**—One of the methods in teaching is to "arouse curiosity that must be met." The continued story that you are reading from week to week stops each time when the curiosity is at its height. Use this plan to gain and hold attention.

3. **Concreteness.**—"Glittering generalities" are seldom very attractive. What man, in general, has done or can or should do, arouses no special interest. But what Abraham Lincoln or William McKinley did is of vital interest. Impersonate ideas in living individuals and you can win and hold attention.

4. **Co-operation.**—Unless a scholar is led to do his share of the work he can not long be interested. A conscientious teacher often does too much for his pupils. No class, of any age, can long be vitally interested, unless kept at work. An interesting teacher always leaves some thinking for his scholars to do.

5. **Contagion.**—The teacher who wishes to interest others must himself be interested. If you are really interested, others will catch it from you.

II. Sensation; Perception; Apperception.

1. **Sensation.**—Sensation is an impression made upon the mind by an outside stimulus. The agents through which sensations are received are called senses. They are taste, smell, touch, hearing and sight.

2. **Perception.**—Perception is the recognition of a sensation.

3. **Apperception.**—Apperception is the "translation and interpretation of the new in terms of the known." It is the clinching of a perception by means of previously acquired knowledge. It is a "spontaneous act of the mind in immediately seeking something in its store of ideas with which to classify a new idea.

Illustration.—When a pin is applied to the end of the finger, an impression is carried through the nerves to the mind. The impression is called a sensation. If this impression is recognized by the mind as having been produced by the pin, that recognition is called **perception.** Apperception is the process of taking this perception and attaching it to and classifying it with similar perceptions already known. Another word for apperception is **assimilation.**

III. Memory; Imagination.

1. **Memory.**—Memory is the power of the mind to retain, recall and recognize. Two aids to memory are (1) repetition and (2) association.

2. **Imagination.**—Imagination is the picture-producing power of

the mind. Professor White defines imagination as "the power of the mind to represent and modify or recombine objects previously known." The wise teacher makes much use of the imagination. "There is no occupation in life," says Professor Roark, "which may not be the better followed with the aid of the imagination. The ditch-digger who can see the effect of his next blow before it is struck; the bricklayer who can see the next brick in position before it is placed; the blacksmith who can shape the bar to the ideal which he projects upon the anvil—these do far better work than those who can see nothing but their memory images or the things actually before them."

In studying history the student should transport himself through imagination into the very life of the events he is studying.

"Ideals are the standards which imagination forms and sets before us as the measure of our conduct."

IV. Feelings; Will.

1. **Feelings.—Feelings are the "mental states of pleasure and pain"** (*Roark*). The teacher should aid the scholar in (1) directing and (2) developing the feelings.

The important place that feelings hold in our actions is strikingly expressed by Patterson DuBois. "Feeling," he affirms, "rules the world. It was not the intellectual convictions alone of Paul, Savonarola, Luther, Knox, Bunyan, Froebel, Wilberforce, Washington, Mrs. Stowe, Whittier and Lincoln, that wrought such reformations, but rather their ardor, their zeal, their courage, their sympathy, their hates and loves, their hopes and fears—in short, those stirrings of the soul which stand immediately behind the will as goads and credentials to action."

2. **Will.—The will is the self-determining power of the mind.** The will is free to choose. Our development is largely due to our choices. "Character may be defined as the sum of our choices." The teacher must not "break" the will of the pupil, but help him to train and develop it.

V. Habit.—Habit is "second nature." Professor Roark says it is "that condition of the mind or body which is manifested in the tendency to unconscious repetition of acts or states." The relation of thoughts, acts, habits, character and destiny are well expressed in these familiar lines:

> "Sow a thought and reap an act;
> Sow an act and reap a habit;
> Sow a habit and reap a character;
> Sow a character and reap a destiny."

BLACKBOARD WORK.

ATTENTION: Foc. Con.	1. Contact. 2. Curiosity. 3. Concreteness. 4. Co-operation. 5. Contagion.
SENSATION: Imp. made upon—. PERCEPTION: Rec. of Sen. APPERCEPTION: Clin. of Per. MEMORY: Ret., Rec., Rec.	IMAGINATION: Pic.-Pro., Pow. FEELINGS: Men. sta. of—. WILL: Self-det., Pow.

TEST QUESTIONS.

1. What three M's should a teacher know?
2. What is attention?
3. Name five methods of securing attention.
4. What is sensation?
5. What is the relation of sensation to perception?
6. Define apperception.
7. What is memory? Give two aids to memory.
8. What is imagination?
9. How does imagination help in studying history?
10. What is the relation of the imagination to our ideals?
11. Define feelings.
12. Define the will. What is character?

LESSON XL. THE ART OF QUESTIONING

1. The efficiency of our teaching depends largely upon the tact and thoroughness with which we put questions. There are two general ways of imparting knowledge: the **lecture** method and the **question** method. The latter method is preferred in instructing children, while a combination of both methods is generally used in teaching adults. The **question** method is often called the "Socratic method," as that way of teaching was so wonderfully used by Socrates.

2. We have called this chapter the art of questioning. It is so, inasmuch as it is largely learned by doing rather than by discussing it. Proficiency in questioning only comes by patient and persistent practice. Go to your classes and learn the art of questioning by **questioning**. Principle as well as practice is involved, however, and it will be wise to consider the general principles which should be kept in view in questioning, and not only **learn how** the successful teacher puts his questions, but **why** one way is better or worse than another.

I. **Kinds of Questions to be Used with Care.**

1. **Rhetorical.**—A rhetorical question is one that does not require an answer in words. The preacher asks, "Who can measure the love of God?" The obvious answer is, "No one"; but he would be wonderfully surprised if some one from his congregation would reply. The rhetorical question is seldom used in teaching.

2. **Elliptical.**—This kind of a question gives a part of the answer and calls upon the scholar to give the rest. Instead of asking, "Where was Jesus born?" the teacher says, "Jesus was born in ——" and leaves the scholar to supply the word "Bethlehem." This sort of questions must be used with great care, as it can so easily be abused by being made too easy. John Adams says, "While a valuable aid with dull and timid children, the elliptical method must not become habitual."

3. **Yes or No.**—Questions that can be answered by "Yes" or "No" are generally condemned. Since there are just two answers, the scholar has an even chance of being correct if he merely guesses. "This criticism is applicable to certain kinds of questions," says

Adams, "but it is often desirable to carry the class with you by getting them to assent to your views, even when you know quite well that you are not testing your pupils. 'Did Joshua despair of conquering Canaan?' is a bad question, if the teacher desires to find out whether the pupil knows the story of the spies. But if the story has been told, and the teacher is applying the lesson, he is quite entitled to ask the question in order to enforce the contrast between the timid spies and the courageous." All rules have exceptions. We must be helped, but not enslaved, by them.

II. **Kind of Questions to be Asked.**

1. **Clear.**—A question should be such that the scholar is sure to know what the question means, whether he knows the answer or not. Often a scholar hesitates to answer, not because he does not know, but because he is uncertain as to what the question means.

2. **Constructive.**—Questions for review may be asked at random, but questions for instruction must be systematic and progressive. Socrates' great power was in that he "never lost sight of the main point, and had a remarkable power of chaining his hearers to the question in hand, and forbidding all discursiveness." The teacher must not forget that, first of all, he is a teacher, and that his questioning is simply to help him in his work as a teacher. If we are constructive in our teaching, we must be constructive in our questioning.

3. **Original.**—The questions in the "lesson helps" are to aid the teacher in the preparation of his lesson, and not to be used by him in testing the scholars. The teacher can soon learn to ask original questions by preparing his lesson so thoroughly that he can teach it with nothing before him except the Bible.

4. **Suggestive.**—Questions should suggest fields of thought to the scholar and set in motion his mental activities. A suggestive question to many scholars would be, "Why didn't Moses lead the Israelites straight from Egypt to Canaan, rather than go many miles out of the direct way?" This question would lead to a study of the physical conditions of the land between Egypt and Canaan.

5. **Spiritual.**—Questions that arouse the conscience and bear upon the character are spiritual. Questions should arouse spiritual as well as mental activities.

III. **Uses of Questions.**

1. **To awaken interest.**—For most minds nothing more quickly arouses and retains the scholar's interest and attention than well-placed questions. Gregory rightly says, "The true stimulant of the human mind is a question." Many classes are killed by too much "talk" and too little questioning.

2. **To aid the memory.**—Questions help the scholar to retain ideas conveyed to him. Information received at the point of a question is likely to stick.

3. **To test the scholar's knowledge.**—Through the lecture method a scholar may conceal his own ignorance and his own knowledge; but "a well-directed question will at once strip off the mask and display the lack of knowledge beneath." For the scholar's

own development it is due him that the teacher ask him judicious questions.

4. **To arouse the scholar's conscience.**—Jesus, our master Teacher, often used this method. To the twelve he said, when others had deserted him, "Would ye also go away?" (John 6: 66-68)—a question that touched the conscience of Peter and caused him to exclaim, "Lord, to whom can we go? thou hast the words of eternal life." Another example is Christ's questions in Matt. 16: 26: "For what shall a man be profited, if he shall gain the whole world, and forfeit his life? or what shall a man give in exchange for his life?"

5. **To test the teacher's work.**—An eminent teacher, in speaking of his use of the question method, said that he first questioned the knowledge into the scholars, and then questioned it out of them. The amount you can question out, will tell you the amount that you were able to question in. The teacher uses review questions to test his work.

It might not be out of place here to note that in another way questions test the teacher's work. A teacher soon reveals to himself whether or not he has a grasp of the lesson by the questions he asks and the way he asks them. The scholars, too, can more easily detect the lack of preparation on the part of the teacher if he uses a question method than if the lecture method be employed.

IV. **Questions Not to Ask.**

1. **Foolish.**—Foolish questions are those that mean very little or nothing; those that bear upon unprofitable themes; and those that will yield to funny answers. "What do you know about Tiglath-Pileser?" asked a teacher of a class of boys in the steam-engine period. "Nothin'," quickly responded one of them. Do not give your scholars an opportunity of being funny at your expense. No matter what grade you are teaching, make your questions mean something.

2. **Catch.**—It is seldom, if ever, necessary in the Bible school, to ask "catch" questions to confuse and humiliate a scholar. Entangling questions have no place in our work. Let your questions be definite and straightforward in their purpose.

3. **Long-answered.**—It is a mistake to ask questions involving long answers. This is especially true in teaching younger scholars. "Give an account of the parable of the talents," is a poor question, because it involves too long an answer. In most cases your questions should demand definite answers.

V. **A Few Suggestions.**

1. Put the element of the unexpected in your questions.

2. Commend all earnest answers, whether right or wrong.

3. Do not question the members of your class in regular rotation.

4. Use all incorrect answers to guide you in your work.

5. Put enthusiasm as well as intelligence in your questions.

6. Begin with simple questions to let the mental machinery get started.

7. Encourage your class to ask questions. Dr. Stalker says,

"Socrates asked questions which his disciples tried to answer. Jesus provoked his disciples to ask questions which he answered."

BLACKBOARD WORK.

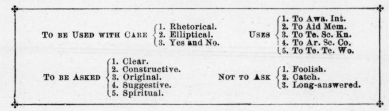

TEST QUESTIONS.

1. Name two general methods used in teaching.
2. Name three kinds of questions to be used with care.
3. Name five kinds of questions to be asked.
4. Name five uses of questions.
5. Name three kinds of questions that should not be asked.
6. What comparison does Dr. Stalker make between Socrates and Jesus?
7. Write out a number of questions at random and then classify them.

LESSON XLI. THE ART OF ILLUSTRATING

1. The word "illustration" comes from a Latin word meaning to light up. An illustration is something that lights up a subject by comparing it with something already known to the scholar.

2. Illustration is based upon the great law of teaching that we must proceed from the concrete to the abstract.

I. **Kinds of Illustrations.**

1. **Material.**—Material illustrations are objects, models of objects, pictures, maps, curios, and such like.

2. **Verbal.**—While material illustrations are often used, the teacher has to depend largely upon verbal or spoken illustrations.

II. **Characteristics of a Good Illustration.**

1. **Must illustrate.**—It must be an outgrowth of the teaching, and not "tacked on." It must be given to make clear an idea, and not for its own sake. A carpenter was once advised to use certain decorations. "That," said the carpenter, "would violate the first rule of architecture. We must never construct ornament, but ornament construction." So it is with the use of illustrations.

2. **Not too much detail.**—Too many details are tiresome, and confuse the mind and prevent it from fixing on the idea to be illustrated.

3. **Intelligible.**—It must come within the circle of knowledge and experience of the scholars. "To compare the unknown with the unknown," well says Professor Gregory, "is to set the blind leading the blind. Of what use is it to talk of Titanic strength to one who never heard of Titans?"

III. **Uses of Illustrations.**

1. **Attract attention.**—The child is caught and held, and the older person "comes back from a mental wandering," at the sound of a story.

2. **Aid the memory.**—Many a sermon or lesson can be recalled by means of a striking illustration. The picture and the object remain in the mind, when abstract statements refuse to stay.

3. **Aid the understanding.**—When Jesus wanted to teach the truth that we are in this world to help others, he gave the illustration of the good Samaritan. Illustrations are invaluable in giving clear conceptions of truths.

4. **Mirror the life.**—The illustration of the prodigal son has mirrored many a wayward boy's life, and brought him back to himself, and to his heavenly Father. Miss Anna Harlow, in approaching her lesson before her primary children one Sunday, told of a boy who threw his shoe at his sister. A little boy from her department went home and told his mother that Miss Harlow accused him of throwing his shoe at his sister. Miss Harlow, of course, did not know that any one before her that morning had done such a thing, but the story mirrored this boy's life, and was just the thing that he needed. A common expression for this use of an illustration is to "awaken the conscience." The young man who is brought home by the story of the prodigal son has had his conscience aroused, as well as the boy in whose experience the shoe story fit so well.

IV. **How to Secure Illustrations.**

1. **Through observation.**—The greatest artists in illustrating are not those that travel the most, but those that see the most when they do travel. Develop the habit of observation.

2. **Through speakers and teachers.**—Notice how others use illustrations. When you hear a good one make a note of it. Study it. Dress it up in your own language, and use it.

3. **Through reading.**—Among books of illustrations we mention five: (1) **The Bible.** For this purpose it is the most prolific of all books. (2) **History and biography.** These will be of special value because they are based upon facts and clothed with real life. (3) **Fiction.** Some of the strongest illustrations may be drawn from this source. (4) **Books of illustrations.** These are helpful, but should be used with care. (5) **Lesson helps.** These are suggestive and practical.

V. **Suggestions for Using Illustrations.**

1. Mix the element of expectation all through your illustrations.

2. Be careful to have a clear idea of the subject to be taught. Get your lesson first, and your illustrations second.

3. Do not press your illustration too far. "No parable goes on all fours."

4. Make your story complete, with beginning, middle and end. Otherwise your scholars may be more interested in the rest of your story than in the idea you are aiming to teach.

5. Do not use too many illustrations. Two illustrations to emphasize one point are likely to neutralize each other.

6. Use the blackboard, pictures and maps freely.
7. Stop when the point is reached.

BLACKBOARD WORK.

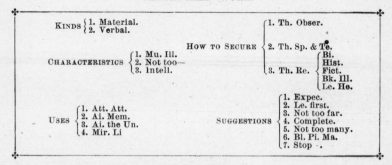

TEST QUESTIONS.

1. What does the word "illustrate" mean?
2. Upon what law of teaching are illustrations based?
3. Name and define two kinds of illustrations.
4. Name three characteristics of a good illustration.
5. Name four uses of illustrations.
6. Name three ways of securing illustrations.
7. Name five kinds of books that are rich in illustrations.
8. State seven suggestions as to the use of illustrations.

LESSON XLII. REVIEW OF THE TEACHER AND HIS WORK

For a review of the teacher and his work, turn to the "Drill Questions" found on pages 112 to 117. Review all of the "Drill Questions" for the final examinations. If you can answer those correctly, you will be sure to pass a successful examination.

PART IX.

EIGHT LESSONS ON THE PUPIL

LESSON XLIII. CHILD NATURE

The object of the Bible-school teacher is to mold character. The impartation of Bible knowledge is a means toward that end. Its work is to be measured, not by what the scholar **knows,** but by what the scholar **does.** He is to judge the impressions he makes by the expressions he receives. To be able to produce the proper expressions from the scholar and thus to mold his life, the teacher must not only know well his Bible and the rules of pedagogy, but the nature of the pupil. He must know the girl as well as the grammar; the boy as well as the Book; the man as well as the method.

There are seven more or less distinct periods in life. The traits of character, the likes and dislikes in one period, are somewhat different from those in any other. True it is that these changes do not come all at once, yet they do come as the child develops from year to year and period to period from infancy to adult life. These seven periods in life are designated in the Bible-school world as cradle roll, beginners, primary proper, junior, intermediate, senior and adult. The ages, roughly speaking, are birth to 3; 3 to 6; 6 to 9; 9 to 12; 12 to 16; 16 to 25; 25 to death.

I. **Methods of Studying Child Nature.**—There are four ways of studying the child:

1. We may treat him as we would an animal; that is, we may examine his outward appearance and notice all of his actions. We may watch him when at work or at play. We may even modify his surroundings and notice the effect of each change. We may experiment with him and find out many things about his nature. With an animal we can go no further than this, as we

93

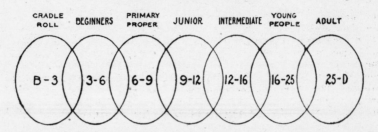

CRADLE ROLL	BEGINNERS	PRIMARY PROPER	JUNIOR	INTERMEDIATE	YOUNG PEOPLE	ADULT
B-3	3-6	6-9	9-12	12-16	16-25	25-D

THE SEVEN PERIODS IN LIFE.

have no means of interpreting his actions by referring them to our own experiences. But with the child it is different. We can penetrate his inner life, for he acts from the motives as we would under the same circumstances.

2. The second means, therefore, of studying child nature is to look into ourselves, and from what we see there, guess what will be found in the child. There is danger, however, in this method, for when we look into ourselves we see the inner life of an adult, which is very different from the inner nature of the child. We must then use the memory, and throw ourselves back to our own days of childhood and try to realize how the child feels and thinks.

3. We may learn much concerning children from well-written books for and about them. Books on the characteristics of the various periods in life and of the various types of mind are to be studiously read.*

4. Much may be learned about children by listening to those who have made a special study of child nature. Excellent addresses are given on this subject at Bible-school conventions, institutes, and summer training-schools.

By these four means, the teacher will little by little learn to know the child he is teaching.

II. **Classification According to Temperament.**—While a more elaborate classification is often made, it will be sufficient here to give the simple twofold division into **motor** and **sensory**.

1. **Motor** children are those who respond easily and quickly to outside influences. They make up their minds quickly, and act forthwith upon whatever conclusion they have made. They are as quick in temper as in intellect. Their anger, however, is of short duration, and they are generally more willing to forgive than the sensory child. Motor children learn quickly, but do not retain so easily. The child with a motor temperament is liable to jump at conclusions, and be more or less fickle.

2. **Sensory** children do not respond to outside influences quickly. They are slow in forming judgments, but these are often sounder than those so quickly reached by the motor children. The sensory children stick to a thing with a greater tenacity. Because of

*A list of books on child nature is given at the close of this lesson.

the apparent slowness, a sensory child is less attractive to the average adult.

A Caution.—A caution is here necessary. The teacher must not expect all children to fall easily and definitely into two groups. Speaking generally, every child is predominately either motor or sensory, but some children have a much more marked bias than others. The types as described above are boldly marked off from one another, but, in actual experience, we find all degrees of gradation between the typically motor on one hand, and the typically sensory on the other. The value of the distinction lies not so much in itself as in the vantage-ground it supplies for studying children. In fact, all such classifications are valuable only in so far as they are applied to and corrected by experience. For example, there is a certain amount of truth in, and a certain amount of instruction to be derived from, the statement sometimes made that girls have usually the motor temperament, and boys the sensory. But to apply this distinction without reference to the individuals of a given class, would be very unwise (*Adams*).

III. **General Characteristics of Children.**

1. **Restlessness.**—This is often treated as a defect, but it is "nature's provision against a one-sided development."

2. **Curiosity.**—This should be stimulated rather than repressed. It is "the gravitation of child life—the motive power on which the teacher must rely" (*Adams*).

3. **Play Instinct.**—This is the key to the secrets of child nature. "It is the spontaneous expression of those very tendencies which education must use" (*Murray*). The little child likes plays that exercise the muscles and satisfy the ear; the boys and girls like games of rivalry; and the youth, games of skill.

4. **Love for Stories.**—A good story will always open the door into the heart of the child. To be a good story-teller is one of the essentials of a good primary teacher.

SEVEN GOOD BOOKS ON CHILD STUDY.

The Study of Child Nature, by Elizabeth Harrison.

From One to Twenty-one, by Walter C. Murray.

Talks with the Training Class, by Margaret Slattery.

The Teacher and the Child, by Thiselton Mark.

The Unfolding Life, by Mrs. Lamoreaux.

Primer on Teaching, by John Adams.

The Pedagogical Bible School, by S. B. Haslett.

BLACKBOARD WORK.

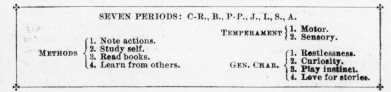

SEVEN PERIODS: C-R., B., P-P., J., I., S., A.

		TEMPERAMENT	1. Motor. 2. Sensory.
METHODS	1. Note actions. 2. Study self. 3. Read books. 4. Learn from others.	GEN. CHAR.	1. Restlessness. 2. Curiosity. 3. Play instinct. 4. Love for stories.

TEST QUESTIONS.

1. What is the object of the Bible-school teacher?
2. Name the seven periods in life and give approximate ages.
3. Name four methods in studying the child.
4. What is the danger in the second method?
5. Name a few good books on child study.
6. Define the motor temperament.
7. Define the sensory temperament.
8. What caution is necessary in making the distinction between the motor and sensory children?
9. Name four general characteristics of children.

LESSON XLIV. THE BEGINNERS: WHO THEY ARE, AND WHAT WE OWE THEM

The beginners are the children in our Bible schools under six years of age. They are the tiny tots who are growing up in every community and looking to the church for their religious training.

I. **Characteristics of the Beginners.**—We must remember in these studies that no two children are exactly alike. We must also not forget that there are certain characteristics that go all the way through the periods of childhood and on into adult life. The trait of curiosity, for instance, is by no means confined to one period in life. But while it is true that no two individuals are alike and that some traits are not confined to definite periods, still each age has some peculiarities which the wise teacher will study, and of which she will take advantage. Some characteristics of the little beginners are:

1. **Physical Restlessness.**—A child in this period can keep still only about ten seconds. Its actions are many times aimless, but they are unceasing. This child should not be compelled to remain long in one position, nor be obliged to keep on the same subject more than ten minutes without some change.

2. **Uncontrolled Imagination.**—The child's imagination is wonderful. To his imagination a stick is a horse, and a row of chairs a railway train. So vivid is his imagination that it sometimes interferes with his conception of the truth. Things seem real to him that are not in reality. Recently a little girl at a breakfast table was given a very small and a large buckwheat cake. Letting her imagination play, she, after eating the little cake, said, "Don't cry, baby, mamma's coming," and then ate the big one.

3. **Inquisitiveness.**—Toward the latter part of this period the child asks questions about everything. His questions are often rambling and disconnected. This characteristic which is now becoming so apparent will get stronger and more logical during the next two periods. The child has everything to learn, and it must learn through putting questions.

4. **Can Not Read.**—The average child under six years of age can not read intelligently. It must therefore be taught without this aid.

5. **Play Instinct.**—Throughout all periods of childhood, the child is fond of play, but in no other period does he play so in-

cessantly. The play of the little beginner often has the element of selfishness, as he has not as yet learned co-operation in playing.

II. **What We Owe the Beginners.**—Considering the characteristics just mentioned, we owe the beginners such things as will properly recognize and utilize them. Some of our debts are:

1. **A Separate Room or Curtained Corner for Class Work.**—The child has eyes that see everything that comes his way.

2. **Suitable Chairs.**—Chairs not too high should be provided.

3. **Suitable Pictures.**—The walls should be covered with the most appropriate pictures, and these should be changed and re-arranged often.

4. **Simple Music.**—This is provided in song-books for the primary departments.

5. **Suitable Plans.**—The plans should, of course, be made and carried out with the traits of the beginners in mind.

6. **Simple Supplemental Work.**—This may be found in Beginners' Supplemental booklets published by various publishing-houses.

7. **Suitable Lessons.**—The International Beginners' Course of two years should certainly be used.

8. **Inspiration.**—Inspiration that they should receive from a consecrated, child-loving teacher.

BLACKBOARD WORK.

CHARACTERISTICS	WHAT WE OWE
1. Phy. Rest.	1. Se. Ro.
2. Unc. Ima.	2. Su. Ch.
3. Inq.	3. Su. Pic.
4. Ca. Re.	4. Si. Mis.
5. Pl. Ins.	5. Su. Pla.
	6. Si. Su. Wo.
	7. Su. Les.
	8. Insp.

TEST QUESTIONS.

1. Name five characteristics of the beginners.
2. Why do some things that are not real seem real to a child?
3. How may the inquisitiveness of the child be best utilized?
4. Name eight things that we owe the beginners.
5. What system of lessons is best fitted for the beginners?

LESSON XLV. THE PRIMARIES: WHO THEY ARE, AND WHAT WE OWE THEM

At about six years of age children enter the public schools. By that time they have developed enough to take a systematic course of instruction. Soon after the child enters the public school he will need to be promoted in the Bible school. His promotion will be from the beginners' class to the primary department proper. This department includes children from six to nine years of age.

I. **Characteristics of the Primary Pupils:**—

1. **Beginning of School Age.**—He may have been in the kindergarten, but his work there was largely wisely directed play. He is now in school with lessons that require him to **study.** His school life brings him into new surroundings, amidst new associates, and these must be recognized by the primary teacher.

2. **Sense Perception.**—In the preparation of her lesson, in its presentation before the class, and in all of the exercises of the primary session, the teacher must not forget that this is the period of sense perception. Especially the senses of sight and hearing must be appealed to in the primary department.

3. **Controlled Imagination.**—We noted in our last lesson that the little beginner had an uncontrolled imagination. So vivid is his imagination that it sometimes interferes with his conception of truth. In the primary age, however, this confusion is past. The imagination in this period is very strong, but under control, and should be appealed to and stimulated.

4. **Curiosity.**—While this trait is by no means confined to the primary children, we mention it here that some suggestions may be made in utilizing it. The wise teacher constantly appeals to the curiosity of her pupils to attract attention, stimulate interest, and impress truth. She covers her picture roll until she is ready to use it. She makes a part of a diagram on the blackboard. She has a box on the desk with a cover on it. The scholars are alert to know what picture is covered, what the remainder of the blackboard outline looks like, and what is in that box. The skillful teacher will be careful to time her words and actions that the picture may be revealed, the blackboard diagram finished and the box uncovered at the proper time to teach and impress the desired lessons.

5. **Imitation.**—Notice that little girl as she goes home from Bible school. What does she do? Tell what the teacher said? Perhaps, but she is more likely to do what the teacher did. She will arrange her dolls as scholars, of which she is the teacher. What does the boy do when he comes home from the circus? Tell about a man walking a tight rope? Yes, but he certainly will fix up a tight rope and try to walk it himself. This imitation is not confined to the primary period, but it is especially strong at the ages of seven and eight.

6. **Desire for Certainty.**—While the child is very credulous, yet the desire for certainty begins to show itself in this period. "Honest," "honor bright," "deed and double," "sure," "honest and true, black and blue; lay me down and cut me in two," are terms often used by these children.

A number of children were playing, and suddenly this conversation took place, as recorded by S. B. Haslett in his **Pedagogical Bible School:**

John—"Where's my knife, Mary."

Mary—"D'now."

John—"You know you have taken it."

Mary—"I haven't got your old knife."

John—"Then you have lost it."

Mary—"I have not had your old knife. So there."

John—"Honor bright?"

Mary—"Honor bright."

John—"Cross your heart?"

Mary—"Cross my heart."

John—"Cross your heart and hope to die?"

Mary—"Cross my heart and hope to die."

John—"Crook your little finger and hope the worms may eat you if you are telling a lie?"

Mary is silent.

John (very slowly and impressively)—"Crook your little finger and hope the worms may eat you if you are telling a lie?"

Mary left the company. She seemed very angry. Presently she returned, threw the knife at her brother, and started away. The children called after her, "Oh, you said 'honor bright' and 'cross my heart.' "

They did not play with her again for a week.

7. **Activity.**—The child of the primary age always wants to be doing something. If he is not given something to do, he will soon find something. Public-school teachers sometimes compel the child to sit absolutely quiet for fifteen minutes or half an hour as a punishment for wrong-doing. Scarcely can a severer punishment be given.

8. **Affection.**—One element that makes primary teaching delightful is the love that the scholars show their teacher. It is the child nature to love. The primary teacher must answer the question: What will the child love? The primary child is not afraid to manifest its affection, as the intermediate child often is.

9. **Limited Vocabulary.**—After the song, "There's a Place in the Ranks for Me," had been used in our primary department, a little girl was overheard by her mother singing, "There's a place in the rags for me." Charley said he always likes to hear them sing the "Dog's holiday" at the church. He meant the "Doxology." In teaching primary children, we must take special care to use words that are understood by the teacher and the scholar in the same sense.

II. **What We Owe the Primary Children:—**

1. **A Suitable Room.**—A separate room, or a room curtained off, where a regular primary program can be used.

2. **Suitable Chairs.**—High benches or chairs are a severe hindrance.

3. **Well-planned Programs.**—Programs where songs, prayers, rest exercises, marches, giving services, supplemental work, etc., etc., are interwoven.

4. **A Graded Department.**—Where the department is of sufficient size, there should be three grades and either three or six classes. Large primary departments will have as many classes as necessary. The larger number of the best organized primary departments have classes that run from six to twelve scholars.

5. **Graded Supplemental Work.**—A definite amount of Scripture, aside from the regular lesson, should be taught each month and each year in this department. Promotions from grade to grade,

and a graduation from the primary to the junior department, are essential.

6. Proper Organization.—A primary superintendent, an organist, a secretary, and a corps of teachers are needed in every well-organized department.

7. Suitable Working Tools.—Some of the tools are a picture roll, primary papers, cabinet of missionary curios and object-lessons, blackboard, piano or organ, case for books and records, and a desk for the secretary. While all of these are not absolutely necessary, better teaching can be done with their aid.

BLACKBOARD WORK.

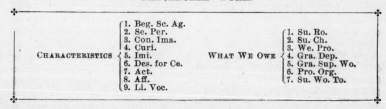

CHARACTERISTICS	WHAT WE OWE
1. Beg. Sc. Ag.	1. Su. Ro.
2. Se. Per.	2. Su. Ch.
3. Con. Ima.	3. We. Pro.
4. Curi.	4. Gra. Dep.
5. Imi.	5. Gra. Sup. Wo.
6. Des. for Ce.	6. Pro. Org.
7. Act.	7. Su. Wo. To.
8. Aff.	
9. Li. Voc.	

TEST QUESTIONS.

1. What ages are included in the primary department proper?
2. Name nine characteristics of the primary pupils.
3. Why should children entering public school be promoted in the Bible school?
4. What two senses are most used by the primary teacher?
5. How may curiosity be used in teaching primary children?
6. How may the pupils' activity be directed in this department?
7. Name six things we owe the primary children.

LESSON XLVI. THE JUNIORS: WHO THEY ARE, AND WHAT WE OWE THEM

The junior department includes those children from nine to twelve years of age. At about nine years of age a gradual change comes over the child's nature. He is manifestly growing away from the things that he loved so much in the first part of his primary period. The motion songs that were once his joy are now a bore. The cradle roll, birthday, and giving exercises in which he once took so much delight now seem to him childish. He is a "big boy" and wants to be treated as such. What may be said of the boy may in a large measure be applied to the girl.

While there are psychological and pedagogical reasons for marking the boundaries of the junior department with the ages nine to twelve, yet we again ask you to remember that no child is one being at the age of eight years and eleven months, and another creature at nine. All that he has learned during the past nine years goes with him into this new period. Many of the characteristics of the beginners' and primary periods run over into the junior period. The restlessness of the beginners' child becomes the activity of the primary pupil and the tremendous energy of the steam-engine boy of the junior department.

I. Characteristics of the Juniors.

1. Reading Period.—The average child at nine years of age is beginning to read with ease. He will read as many story-books as come his way. When the child enters the junior department the teacher should take advantage of his desire for reading by telling him where to find excellent stories in the Bible, and by giving him a chance to tell about what he has read. This is the time when each pupil should have a Bible of his very own, and he should be drilled in turning to various parts of it where splendid stories and interesting parables are found.

2. Steam-engine Period.—Charlie, while playing in the living-room, gave a tremendous yell. His mother hurried in from the kitchen, anxiously asking, "What's wrong?" "Oh, nothing, mother, but I'd died if I hadn't got to yell." The children of this period want to run rather than walk. They want games that are strenuous and that present opportunities to take risks. The boys do not want to be referred to as "little children," nor do they want childish games. Juniors love outdoor exercise, for it gives them opportunity to utilize this great store of energy.

3. Inquisitive Period.—This trait that was much in evidence in the beginners' and primary periods now reaches its climax. He wants to know why a crawfish goes backward, why a rooster flaps his wings before he crows, and why the chickens don't fall off the roost when they go to sleep. He will notice inconsistencies and put questions that beggar all answers. He loves to scratch off all veneering and reveal the real material inside.

4. Friendly Period.—Every boy has his chum and every girl her friend. These companions want to be together all the time, and never tire of each other. In this period, boys do not care to play with girls, but boys want to be with boys only, and girls with girls only. The club spirit begins here. The girls have "societies" and the boys "gangs."

5. Memory Period.—In his book, After the Primary, What? A. H. McKinney tells of an old man who frequently said to his wife, "I knew that when I was ten years of age." So very frequently did he say this that his wife one day pointedly said, "It's a pity that you never learned anything since you were ten." While this was said in a joking manner, yet there is philosophy beneath it. While he had learned many things in adult life, he remembered most distinctly those things that he had learned in the memory period. The junior teacher has the pupils when the memory is "most impressionable and most tenacious." It is a sin for parents and teachers to permit children to pass this period without literally saturating them with outlines of Old and New Testament history, and many of the choicest passages of the Bible.

6. Habit-forming Period.—This is the time when the boys and girls are trying to do almost everything they see older folks doing. Such habits as swearing, smoking, stealing, etc., are often begun at this time.

It is also the habit-forming period in a good sense. During these junior years the children should form the habit, if not already acquired, of daily Bible reading, daily prayer, attending the preaching services, and systematic giving.

A QUESTION AND ITS ANSWER.—The important and natural question is: How may the teacher of juniors, with the short time that she has in which to influence them, accomplish anything definite in regard to so many habits? The answer is, Almost everything will depend upon the action of the teacher and those associated with her in the conduct of the class or the department. In other words: The leaders must create and maintain an atmosphere that will tend to the formation of correct habits. The power of a proper Bible-school atmosphere, backed by the lives of the leaders in the school work, can not be rated too highly (*McKinney*).

Be what you wish your scholars to be.

7. **Fruitful Period.**—Of all the seven periods of life, the junior furnishes the richest harvest of spiritual results. Children who have been taught well in the homes and in the Bible schools will naturally want to make a confession of their faith in Christ and surrender their lives to him sometime between the ages of nine and thirteen. The wise superintendent of the junior department will see that the proper Scriptures are taught during this period, that the child may understand how to become a Christian and how to live a Christian life.

II. **What We Owe the Juniors.**

1. **An Organized Junior Department.**—It has often been said that the primary child, when graduated, comes out of the hotbed of a well-organized primary department into the cold refrigerator of the poorly organized "main school." No wonder many of our junior children have been "frozen" out. Every school owes the juniors a well-organized department. This department is possible even where no separate room can be given to them. (See p. 76.)

2. **His Own Bible.**—A good custom has grown up in many schools of presenting to each primary graduate a good Bible. Where this is not done, some arrangement should be made to make it possible for each junior pupil to own his Bible. Generally it is not best to give Bibles outright. Have the scholars earn them by work done, or buy them.

3. **Tables for Manual Work.**—The juniors ought to be taught to make outline maps, pulp maps, write histories of men, and make illustrated scrap-books. A lap-board may be used where the room is seated with pews.

4. **Graded Supplemental Work.**—As this is the memory period, some graded supplemental work should furnish material to be memorized. A definite amount of work should be arranged for each month and each year.

5. **Suitable Reading.**—As the average child reads easily at this period, he should be directed to read the right kind of stories. He is sure to read, so the problem of the teacher is, "*What* shall he read?"

6. **Suitable Work.**—The boys and girls in the steam-engine

period must do something. The wise junior teacher will take advantage of this, and organize the boys into messenger corps and the girls into sunshine bands, thus giving them the opportunity of carrying messages to the Home Department members and to the absentees, bearing flowers to the shut-ins and to the sick. Social evenings and entertainments that are both instructive and fascinating should be provided.

7. **Adaptation of Lessons.**—Whatever lessons may be taught to the juniors, they should be adapted to the characteristics mentioned above. The junior child should neither be taught as the primary. nor as the intermediate pupils are. Study what the children like, and then present the lesson, using that as an approach.

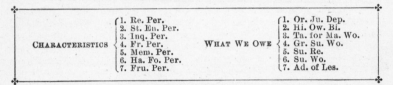

BLACKBOARD WORK.

| CHARACTERISTICS | 1. Re. Per.
2. St. En. Per.
3. Inq. Per.
4. Fr. Per.
5. Mem. Per.
6. Ha. Fo. Per.
7. Fru. Per. | WHAT WE OWE | 1. Or. Ju. Dep.
2. Hi. Ow. Bi.
3. Ta. for Ma. Wo.
4. Gr. Su. Wo.
5. Su. Re.
6. Su. Wo.
7. Ad. of Les. |

TEST QUESTIONS.

1. What ages are included in the junior period?
2. Why is the junior department necessary?
3. Name seven characteristics of the juniors.
4. Name seven things that we owe the juniors.
5. What steps would you take in organizing a junior department?
6. What is manual work?
7. What is graded supplemental work?
8. Why is this called the fruitful period?

LESSON XLVII. THE INTERMEDIATES: WHO THEY ARE, AND WHAT WE OWE THEM

Adolescence is "the period of human life that lies between puberty and the time at which the body acquires full development." Adolescence is often divided into three stages: Early adolescence, from twelve to sixteen years of age; middle adolescence, from sixteen to twenty; later adolescence, from twenty to twenty-four. The intermediate department in our Bible schools covers the first of these stages. This is the period of the transformation of the boy to a man, of the girl to a woman.

The importance of the period of adolescence is well expressed by S. B. Haslett in his **Pedagogical Bible School:** "Life," he says, "seems to center in adolescence. Childhood looks forward to this period and is preparatory to it. Mature life receives its setting and character from adolescence. This is the golden period of life. Soul and body reach their largest and most rapid development here. The treasures of the past here are poured out in extravagant profusion, as if this was nature's supreme and final effort to be comprehensive and universal. The future of the race is insured by endowing the individual at that point in his career when his character, worth and activity count most for future generations. The future man will be as was his adolescence. The future race will be as was its youth."

I. **Characteristics of the Intermediates.**—It is difficult to state the characteristics of the intermediate pupils, as they are so different in different individuals. All rules made for this period are burdened with exceptions. This is a stage of "exceptions to the rule." Those characteristics, however, that stand out most prominent are:

1. **Rapid Physical Growth.**—From twelve to fourteen years of age is the time of the greatest growth in girls and from fourteen to sixteen in boys. Girls and boys of this period grow seven, eight and even eleven inches in one year. Because of this rapid physical growth, it is the awkward age. It is the period when girls let dishes fall, and boys fall over chairs. This physical transition manifests itself in giggling, crude jokes, blushing, loud talking, boisterous actions, and sometimes laziness.

2. **Keen Sense of Humor.**—Boys and girls of this period are especially fond of funny stories. Then, too, things are funny to them that are a bore to adults. The boy delights in removing the chair from under another boy; he finds much pleasure in mussing his chum's hair, knocking his hat off, or tripping him. Teachers who do not appreciate the "rude" fun of the intermediates do not get into their inner lives.

3. **Keen Sense of Honor.**—Pupils of this period generally will not tell on each other. A girl of this period was asked to choose between telling on one of her playmates or taking a whipping. She chose the latter. The practical thought here for the teacher is this: Don't ask your intermediate scholars to tell on each other. This dawning of the sense of honor should be fully recognized and developed.

4. **Love of the Thrilling.**—This is the time when "blood and thunder" stories are in demand. Boys demand stories filled with daring activity and hazardous adventure. Girls take great pleasure in reading books written for the boys, as well as those written for themselves. Boys care little or nothing for girls' books and papers.

5. **New Religious Experiences.**—Well-graded schools lead most of the pupils to Christ during the latter part of the junior period. The intermediate scholar is therefore undergoing new religious experiences. He is forming his Christian character in a most definite way. This is the period when "right and wrong, strength and strategy, emotion and intelligence, religion and indifference, vice and virtue, egoism and altruism, all seem to be engaged in a conflict as complex as it is severe, as vital and momentous as it is mysterious and necessary" (*Haslett*). Dr. Morro made a study of three thousand students in academies in Italy, and found that conduct is good at eleven, but fell way down at the lowest point at fourteen, and then gradually rose until the highest point was reached at

eighteen. This study shows us how important it is to lead children to Christ in the junior period, and how critical is the intermediate period.

6. **Hero Worship.**—At this time every boy has his hero and every girl her heroine. These ideal personages have much to do in the molding of character. Find the boy's hero and you have found the "point of contact." This hero may be a pugilist, a soldier, an inventor or an outlaw. Pictures and books have much to do in the formation of heroes and heroines in the minds of these intermediates.

7. **Fighting.**—This characteristic is confined almost exclusively to the boy. At this time he is likely to cause more real commotion and trouble than in any other period from infancy to adult life. He would "rather fight than eat." If he can not find some one to fight, he will encourage smaller ones to enter into a "scrap." Fight he wants and fight he must have. I asked the intermediate boys of a Y. M. C. A. in an Ohio city what they thought of a fellow who wouldn't fight. Here are some of the answers received: "He's no good;" "He isn't game;" "He ought to be made to fight;" "He's a big coward." About 90 per cent. of the boys said in their own original way that the boy who wouldn't fight was "no good."

What are we going to do with this "fighting boy"? Some teachers say: "You can not do anything with him;" "There's no use trying;" "They are genuinely bad;" etc., etc. But this boy is not hopeless. That characteristic which manifests itself in this unpleasant way is a virtue wrongly directed. The "fighting" period shows the **dawning of the sense of heroism.** The boy wants to be a hero, and he falsely thinks that "fighting" is the best way to express this desire. Show the boy that it is more **heroic** not to fight than to fight, and you can not compel him to fight.

II. **What We Owe the Intermediates.**

1. **Intermediate Teachers.**—Teachers who understand that these boys and girls are neither children nor adults; teachers who know why the pupils giggle and blush and act boisterously; teachers who will neither call them bad nor treat them as bad; teachers who appreciate the criticalness of their physical and spiritual life of this period of transition.

2. **Teachers of the Same Sex.**—Generally speaking, it is better for men to teach boys and women to teach girls in this department. There are, however, many exceptions to this rule. A woman of strong personality is much better than a man with neither enthusiasm nor inspiration.

3. **Suitable Reading.**—Since these girls and boys demand stories that are filled with daring deeds and heroic adventure, this should be supplied by the Bible schools. The pupils of this period will read, and it depends upon the teachers as to whether this reading shall be of the bad heroic or of the noble heroic.

4. **Supplemental Lessons.**—Aside from the regular lessons, supplemental work should be introduced that will present the great biographies of the Bible.

5. **Organized Classes.**—This is the "team" period, when the

boys and girls work as a body, and not alone as individuals. Take advantage of this team spirit, and the desire to run their own affairs, and organize them for service. Boys of this period can often govern themselves to the satisfaction of the school better than the teacher can control them.

6. **Suitable Social Life.**—Invite your scholars to your home, and entertain them according to their characteristics. Visit the ball field with the boys and go walking with the girls. In short, direct the games and recreations of your pupils.

7. **Close Friend.**—Each intermediate wants a close friend. Outside of his home, this friend should be his Bible-school teacher. His teacher will watch for the crises of his pupil's experiences and help him to choose the proper paths. He will guide his spiritual life through this dangerous period. He will help him not only to choose, but to keep Christ as his hero.

BLACKBOARD WORK.

CHARACTERISTICS	1. Ra. Phy. Gro. 2. Ke. Se. Hu. 3. Ke. Se. Ho. 4. Lo. of Thr. 5. New Re. Ex. 6. He. Wor. 7. Fight.	WHAT WE OWE	1. Int. Tea. 2. Tea. Sa. Sex. 3. Su. Re. 4. Su. Les. 5. Or. Cl. 6. Su. So. Li. 7. Cl. Fr.

TEST QUESTIONS.

1. Define adolescence.
2. Name five characteristics of the intermediate pupil.
3. Why do most boys in the later part of intermediate period want to fight?
4. Name five things we owe the intermediates.
5. What kind of supplemental lessons should the intermediates have?
6. Why are organized classes advisable in this period?

LESSON XLVIII. THE YOUNG PEOPLE: WHO THEY ARE, AND WHAT WE OWE THEM

The adult department of the International Sunday-school Association includes all persons over sixteen years of age. This department covers what has generally been called the senior department, and also the adult department proper. Where the Bible schools are organized according to the International plan, the adult department naturally divides itself into two parts:

1. **The Senior or Young People's Division** (including those from sixteen to twenty-five or thirty years of age).

2. **The Older Adult Division or Adult Division Proper** (including those from twenty-five or thirty to death). In this lesson we take up the first of these parts.

I. **Characteristics of Young People or Seniors.**

1. **Strong Intellect.**—The powers of rational thought are now rapidly developing. The individuals are getting their bearings and are thinking about the things of life. The sterner and deeper

things are taking hold and demanding consideration. Some of the world's greatest thinkers have done their greatest work before they reached the age of twenty-five. Shelling was recognized as a philosopher at twenty-one; Kant began his literary career at twenty-two, and Aristotle at the age of sixteen began the study of philosophy under Plato. The sudden changes in the mental nature that characterized the intermediate period have now gradually given place to a steady development of intellectual powers.

2. **Investigative.**—In the previous periods of life the scholar is more or less likely to leap at conclusions when only a part of the evidence has been produced. In this department, however, it requires more to persuade him. He demands that all sides of the question be presented. He is more thorough in his investigation of evidence.

3. **Strong Sense of Honor.**—The young people's sense of honor must be respected if they are won to that which is best and most useful in the industrial and religious life. The following incident given in the **Pedagogical Bible School** will emphasize this fact: "I remember a young man whose father came to me many years ago, and he said: 'My son is utterly worthless. I can't do anything with him. He won't work. He won't study. He won't do anything. He is bound to be idle, and I can't help it.' I said, 'Send him to me.' The boy came. He was nineteen years old. It was rather late, but I took him into my room and I said, 'Look here; you know I think a great deal of you'—and I meant what I said. 'I think you have splendid ability. I think you can do almost anything you have a mind to do. I think you have the best opportunity to give a surprise to the community that you live in of any man in this world.' He looked at me. I said: 'You have reached pretty near the bottom. Your chances are growing less every day. There is only one thing for you to do, and that is to right about face and do your duty, and be a man.' We both sat silent. We had a sort of Quaker meeting. I said: 'I want you to go into that Latin grammar class and lead it, and do your work, and I want to be the man to proclaim what you have done when you have done it. I want you to stand by it, and we will see if you and I together can not accomplish it. I want you to lead it.' He did lead it. He came out all right. When he was ready for college I said: 'You are going to college now. I have not said much to you, but I am proud of you, and everybody else is getting so. When you enter that class in college do you lead it! Cut every bridge behind you and lead that class.' . . . I meant what I said to him. And he did it. It won't do to go much further; you know the man. One day Mr. Whittier wrote to me and he said: 'They want a man for so and so.' I said: 'There he is.' They took him. He is one of the best paid teachers in this country, and his name is known on both sides of the water. . . . I did not make him, but, oh, I was in earnest with that fellow" (*Augustine Jones, New England Association of Colleges and Preparatory Schools, School Review*).

4. **Homing Instinct.**—In the intermediate stage the youths of both sexes were interested in anything that related to the opposite

sex. But such interest was more or less superficial, and gave occasion for slighting and trivial remarks. Little, if any, seriousness was felt when questions relating to marriage and home were discussed. At the close of the intermediate period, however, the homing faculty is ripe for development. The realities concerning married life now take a deeper hold. There is a danger here in that the obligations of home life will be assumed too early; that the responsibilities of conjugal life be taken before maturity is attained. This is the period of desire for social gatherings and parties where young men and young women are together.

5. **Sensitive to Public Opinion.**—What other people think is a matter of greatest consideration. The intermediate boy cares little for the opinions of others, but now many things are done or left undone largely because of public opinion.

6. **Clear Sense of Right and Wrong.**—While many of the rough and impetuous characteristics of the intermediate stage are still present at this time, yet we see the manly and womanly elements manifesting themselves. The young people desire the best and the highest. They generally have a clear sense of right and wrong, whether they exercise it or not. Conscience speaks with great power, and influences the life. Appeals may be made to high principles and lofty standards of character.

On the other hand, this is the period in life when the most criminals are made. Train wreckers, burglars and robbers are often under twenty years of age.

7. **Life of Joy.**—Young people seem to live to have a good time. Nature is generous with them. They overflow with enthusiasm for real fun. They enjoy life to the full. Hope and joy come naturally. This life of joy is divinely intended, but it must be guided by teachers who understand the divine will in the shaping of these happy, hopeful lives.

III. **What We Owe the Young People.**

1. **Organized Classes.**—Every Bible school should have one or more organized classes. Where the school is large enough, there should be one class for young men and another for young women, and a mixed class for the older adults. These classes should have a teacher, president, vice-president, secretary, treasurer, and at least three committees: Lookout, Social and Devotional. Classes now may be larger than in the previous department. The size of the class will likely be limited only by the size of the teacher and of the room space.

2. **Proper Religious Atmosphere.**—Many schools do very little in atmosphering the young people. How can this be done?

(1) By having at least a half-dozen people at the door each Sunday morning ready to greet all comers. A hearty handshake from one is good, but from a half-dozen is better.

(2) By a letter sent by the teacher on Monday morning to each new scholar, renewing the welcome of the class and the school.

(3) By informal socials where the programs are arranged to meet the characteristics of this department.

(4) By permitting no one to be a stranger more than once. Put

each new scholar to work immediately. No man can keep his religion unless he uses it.

(5) By having teachers who love both Christ and men.

3. **A Training-class.**—Many of the scholars of this period will desire to take up special training that they may better serve their master Teacher. To this end a teacher-training class should be organized each year. When each class graduates, an appropriate recognition service should be held.

BLACKBOARD WORK.

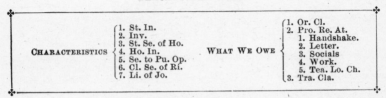

CHARACTERISTICS	{	1. St. In.
		2. Inv.
		3. St. Se. of Ho.
		4. Ho. In.
		5. Se. to Pu. Op.
		6. Cl. Se. of Ri.
		7. Li. of Jo.
			WHAT WE OWE	{	1. Or. Cl.
					2. Pro. Re. At.
					  1. Handshake.
					  2. Letter.
					  3. Socials
					  4. Work.
					  5. Tea. Lo. Ch.
					3. Tra. Cla.

TEST QUESTIONS.

1. Name the two natural divisions of the adult department.
2. Name five characteristics of the young people.
3. Name three things that we owe the young people.
4. How can we surround them with the proper religious atmosphere?
5. Define an organized class.

LESSON XLIX. THE OLDER ADULTS: WHO THEY ARE, AND WHAT WE OWE THEM

In our last lesson we noted that the adult department naturally divided itself into two parts: (1) The Senior or Young People's Division, and (2) The Older Adult Division. In this lesson the second of these parts is discussed.

I. **Characteristics of the Older Adults.**

1. **Patriotism.**—This is a characteristic that reaches its highest and truest power in this period.

2. **Reflective Powers.**—The older people look back through memory's window and re-enjoy the activities of the past. To shut off what "has been" from the adult is to take away one of his best sources of joy.

3. **Love of Quiet Conversation.**—In social functions that bring the young people together, plans of entertainment must be provided. The adults, however, are contented to sit and talk quietly for hours concerning current and other topics.

4. **Home-centered.**—Fathers and mothers find their lives largely centered in the members of the home circle. They are literally living for their children, and find joy in serving them.

5. **Love for Humanity.**—The altruistic spirit which began to manifest itself in the intermediate period and became stronger among the young people is now reaching its largest field of useful-

ness. The adult is interested in missions (both foreign and home), in the state, in the public schools, and in all that relates to the general welfare of mankind.

6. **A Sense of Leadership and Example.**—The adult feels his power as a leader, and realizes his duty as one who is marking out a path for others.

7. **Executive Ability.**—Governors, lawyers, presidents and heads of large business concerns are in this department of life.

II. **What We Owe the Older Adults.**

1. **Capable Teachers.**—One reason that adults have not attended the Bible school in larger numbers is because the teachers were not making the lessons interesting. Recently some members of adult classes were asked to state why more adults did not attend the Bible school. Here are some of the answers: "The teacher argues too much;" "The teacher is too 'preachified';" "The teacher gives too much chaff, and not enough wheat;" "The teacher treats us as children." We owe the adult, teachers who are Bible students, good organizers, and enthusiastic leaders.

2. **Organized Classes.**—The older adults want to work systematically. This is only possible by organizing for service. From each class should be selected a president, vice-president, secretary, treasurer, and as many committees as the local needs demand. Books are now on sale that give many "ways of working" for the organized adult classes.

3. **Suitable Classrooms.**—The adult class can not do its best work in a room with many other classes. Where a separate room is possible it should by all means be occupied. Many adult classes go to other buildings near the church for the half-hour Bible study, meeting in the opening and closing exercises with the other classes of the school. Where a separate room in the church or near the church is not possible, curtain off a section of your large room for your class.

4. **An Opportunity for Adequate Christian Service.**—This is supplied by the modern adult Bible class. Men will leave home and business, work for meager wages, live for many days on little or no food, sleep on the frozen ground, endure the hardships of march and battle, to fight for their country. Such a cause challenges their best efforts. When men realize that the organized Bible class presents an opportunity for service adequate to their powers, they will leave business and social engagements, and all other things necessary, to champion such a cause.

BLACKBOARD WORK.

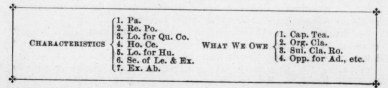

CHARACTERISTICS	WHAT WE OWE
1. Pa. 2. Re. Po. 3. Lo. for Qu. Co. 4. Ho. Ce. 5. Lo. for Hu. 6. Se. of Le. & Ex. 7. Ex. Ab.	1. Cap. Tea. 2. Org. Cla. 3. Sui. Cla. Ro. 4. Opp. for Ad., etc.

TEST QUESTIONS.

1. Name seven characteristics of the older adults.
2. Which one of these characteristics do you think is strongest in men?
3. Which of these characteristics is strongest in women?
4. Name four things that we owe the adults.
5. Name some qualifications of a successful teacher of adults.
6. How would you proceed in organizing an adult class?
7. Where a separate classroom is not possible, what is the next best thing?
8. How does the adult Bible class furnish opportunities for unlimited Christian service?

LESSON L. A CHART STORY

IN YOUR REVIEW, USE QUESTIONS 269-289, AS FOUND IN THE LATTER PART OF THE BOOK.

WHO THEY ARE, AND WHAT WE OWE THEM.

	BEGINNERS.	PRIMARIES.	JUNIORS.
WHO THEY ARE.	1. Physical Restlessness. 2. Uncontrolled Imagination. 3. Inquisitiveness. 4. Can Not Read. 5. Play Instinct.	1. Beginning of School Age. 2. Sense Perception. 3. Controlled Imagination. 4. Curiosity. 5. Imitation. 6. Desire for Certainty. 7. Activity. 8. Affection. 9. Limited Vocabulary.	1. Reading Period. 2. Steam-engine Period. 3. Inquisitive Period. 4. Friendly Period. 5. Memory Period. 6. Habit-forming Period. 7. Fruitful Period.
WHAT WE OWE THEM.	1. Separate Room. 2. Suitable Chairs. 3. Suitable Pictures. 4. Simple Music. 5. Suitable Plans. 6. Simple Supplemental Work. 7. Suitable Lessons. 8. Inspiration.	1. Suitable Room. 2. Suitable Chairs. 3. Well-planned Programs. 4. Graded Department. 5. Graded Supplemental Work. 6. Proper Organization. 7. Suitable Working Tools.	1. An Organized Dept. 2. Their Own Bibles. 3. Tables for Manual Work. 4. Graded Supplemental Work. 5. Suitable Reading. 6. Suitable Work. 7. Adaptation of Lessons.

	INTERMEDIATES.	YOUNG PEOPLE AND	OLDER ADULTS.
WHO THEY ARE.	1. Rapid Physical Growth. 2. Keen Sense of Humor. 3. Keen Sense of Honor. 4. Love of the Thrilling. 5. New Religious Experiences. 6. Hero Worship. 7. Fighting.	1. Strong Intellect. 2. Investigative. 3. Strong Sense of Honor. 4. Homing Instinct. 5. Sensitive to Public Opinion. 6. Clear Sense of Right and Wrong. 7. Life of Joy.	1. Patriotism. 2. Reflective Powers. 3. Love for Quiet Conversation. 4. Home-centered. 5. Love for Humanity. 6. Sense of Leadership. 7. Executive Ability.
WHAT WE OWE THEM.	1. Intermediate Teachers. 2. Teachers of the Same Sex. 3. Suitable Reading. 4. Supplemental Lessons. 5. Organized Classes. 6. Suitable Social Life. 7. Close Friend.	1. Organized Classes. 2. Proper Religious Atmosphere. 3. A Training-class.	1. Capable Teachers. 2. Organized Classes. 3. Suitable Class Rooms. 4. Opportunity for Service.

DRILL QUESTIONS

IN NINE PARTS.

Those who are able to answer all of these "Drill Questions" need have no fear of the final examination. These are not given to save study, but to direct your study and make it definite. From these 289 questions your examination questions will largely be taken. These questions may be used on the plan of the old-fashioned "Spelling Bee," as well as in concert drill, and in individual oral and written tests.

Part I. The Bible and Its Books.

1. What does the word "Bible" mean?
2. Give two names of the Bible found in the Book itself.
3. Name the two divisions of the books of the Bible.
4. How many books in the Old Testament?
5. How many books in the New Testament?
6. How many books in the entire Bible?
7. Name the divisions of the books of the Old Testament.
8. How many books of the Law are there? Of History? Of Devotion? Of the Major Prophets? Of the Minor Prophets?
9. Name the books of the Law.
10. Name the books of History.
11. Name the books of Devotion.
12. Name the books of the Major Prophets.
13. Name the books of the Minor Prophets.
14. Name the divisions of the books of the New Testament.
15. How many books of Biography are there? Of History? Of Special Letters? Of General Letters? Of Prophecy?
16. Name the books of Biography.
17. Name the book of History.
18. Name the Special Letters.
19. Name the General Letters.
20. Name the book of Prophecy.
21. Name the book written by Matthew.
22. Name the book written by Mark.
23. Name the books written by Luke.
24. Name the books written by John.
25. Who wrote the Special Letters?
26. Name the books written by the following persons: **(1)** Peter; **(2)** James; (3) Jude.
27. Name the "synoptic Gospels."
28. Give the names of the Gospel writers who were apostles.

Part II. Evidences.

29. Give five reasons why you believe the Bible is the word of God.
30. Give five reasons for believing that Jesus is the Christ, the Son of God.

Part III. Old Testament History.

31. Name in order sixteen leading characters of Old Testament history.
32. Who was the first murderer?
33. Who was the first martyr?
34. Give the names of Noah's three sons.
35. What relation was Lot to Abraham?
36. Name the sons of Jacob and Leah.
37. Name the sons of Jacob and Rachel.
38. Name the sons of Jacob and Bilhah.
39. Name the sons of Jacob and Zilpah.
40. In what country was Moses born?
41. On what mountain did he die?

42. Who was Moses' successor?
43. What rule follows Joshua's death?
44. Who was the strongest judge physically?
45. What judge was a woman?
46. Who was the last judge?
47. How many judges were there?
48. Who was the first king of the Jews?
49. Who anointed the first king as king?
50. Who was the second king of the Jews?
51. By whom was the second king anointed?
52. Who was the third king of the Jews?
53. At the death of what king was the Jewish kingdom divided?
54. When the kingdom was divided, what was the northern part called?
55. Who was the first king of Israel?
56. When the kingdom was divided, what was the southern part called?
57. Who was the first king of Judah?
58. Name the six divisions of Old Testament history.
59. Give the extent of the period of Probation.
60. Give the extent of the period of Preparation.
61. Give the extent of the period of Conquest.
62. Give the extent of the period of Power.
63. Give the extent of the period of Decline.
64. Give the extent of the period of Servitude.
65. How many centuries between the Old and New Testaments?
66. Name three events in the period of Probation.
67. Name three events in the period of Preparation.
68. Name three events in the period of Conquest.
69. Name three events in the period of Power.
70. Name five epochs in the period of Servitude.
71. Name two epochs in the period of Decline.
72. Name two persons in the period of Probation.
73. Name two persons in the period of Preparation.
74. Name four persons in the period of Conquest.
75. Name three persons in the period of Power.
76. Name three persons in the period of Decline.
77. Name five persons in the period of Servitude.
78. Give the dates of the following events: (1) Fall of Samaria; (2) Babylonian captivity; (3) Return from Babylonian captivity.
79. Who led the Israelites across the Red Sea?
80. Who led the Israelites across the Jordan River?
81. Name four of the greatest "Judges."
82. When did the kingdom of Israel end?
83. Who was the "gospel" prophet?
84. Who was the "weeping" prophet?
85. Who was the Persian ruler who permitted the Jews to return to Jerusalem
86. Of what kingdom was Alexander the Great a ruler?
87. What man led in a revolt against the Grecian government for the sake of the Jews and the Jewish religion?
88. Of what kingdom was Herod the Great a ruler?
89. What relation was the Herod at the time of the birth of Christ to Herod the Great?

PART IV. NEW TESTAMENT HISTORY.

90. Name the three divisions of New Testament history.
91. Name seven periods in the life of Christ.
92. Name five events in the period of Preparation.
93. Name five events in the First Year of Christ's ministry.
94. Name five events in the Second Year.
95. Name five events in the Third Year.
96. Name five events in the Last Three Months.
97. Name five events in the Last Week.
98. Name five events in the Forty Days.

99. Name in order thirty-five events in the life of Christ.
100. In what city was Jesus born?
101. To what country was he taken when but a baby? Why?
102. Where was Jesus' home after he was brought back from Egypt?
103. Who baptized Jesus?
104. In what river was Jesus baptized?
105. What did a voice out of heaven say when Christ was baptized?
106. In what place was Christ's first miracle performed?
107. How many times did Christ cleanse the temple?
108. With what person was Christ's first recorded discourse?
109. What is the first year of Christ's public ministry often called?
110. With what lake are many of the events of Christ's life connected?
111. What Gospel writer gives the longest account of the "Sermon on the Mount"? (Matthew).
112. Near what city did Christ raise from the dead the only son of a widow?
113. In what city did Christ raise from the dead the daughter of Jairus?

114. What is the second year of Christ's ministry sometimes called?
115. What great miracle is recorded by all the Gospel writers?
116. What was Peter's confession?
117. Where is Peter's confession found?
118. What did God say concerning Christ at the Transfiguration?
119. What Gospel writer alone records the parable of the good Samaritan?

120. What is the third year of Christ's ministry sometimes called?
121. What man climbed up a tree to see Christ?
122. On what day was Christ's triumphal entry into Jerusalem?
123. In what city was the memorable "upper room"?
124. What ordinance of the church was instituted in the "upper room"?

125 Name the periods in Christ's life when he: (1) First cleansed the temple; (2) Discoursed with Nicodemus; (3) Was baptized; (4) Delivered the "Sermon on the Mount"; (5) Raised the widow's son; (6) Fed the 5,000; (7) Raised Jairus' Daughter; (8) Was anointed by Mary; (9) Gave the parable of the Ten Virgins; (10) Was transfigured; (11) Gave the parable of the good Samaritan; (12) Ascended; (13) Instituted the Lord's Supper; (14) Talked with the woman of Samaria.
126. Name six persons whom you consider the greatest in New Testament history, not including Jesus.
127. Name three homes of Jesus.
128. By whom was Jesus buried?
129. What noted man helped to bury Jesus?
130. Name two periods of "the Beginnings of the Church."
131. When did the church begin? (181)
132. With what person did it begin among the Gentiles?
133. How many of the apostles died a martyr's death?
134. Name two hypocrites in the early church.
135. Name five events connected with the church at Jerusalem.
136. Name three men that had much to do with the spread of the early church.
137. Name six periods in the life of Paul.
138. In what city was Paul born?
139. To what city did he go when he was still in his teens? (Jerusalem).
140. Who was his teacher in Jerusalem?
141. Who was the first Christian martyr?
142. What important young man witnessed Stephen's death?
143. Name three places in the Bible where Paul's conversion is recorded.

144. How many missionary journeys did Paul make?
145. Name three of Paul's traveling companions.
146. Whom does Paul call his "child in faith"?
147. Name two cities in which Paul was in prison.

148. Under the reign of what man did Paul meet his death?
149. Name the three dispensations of Bible history.
150. Concerning the dispensations give the extent: (1) Of the Patriarchal; (2) of the Jewish; (3) of the Christian.
151. What was the institution of worship under the Patriarchal dispensation?

152. What were the three institutions under the Jewish dispensation?
153. What is the institution of the worship under the Christian dispensation?

PART V. BIBLE GEOGRAPHY.

154. Name three Bible rivers.
155. Locate (1) the Nile; (2) the Euphrates; (3) the Jordan.
156. Into what sea does the Nile flow?
157. Into what gulf does the Euphrates flow?
158. Through what lake does the Jordan flow?
159. Into what sea is the Jordan lost? (213)
160. What sea did the Israelites cross in their flight from Egypt?
161. Name five Bible mountains. (215)
162. Locate the following mountains: (1) Sinai; (2) Nebo; (3) Carmel; (4) Hermon; (5) Olives.
163. Name three Bible cities that begin with B.
164. Locate (1) Babylon; (2) Bethlehem; (3) Bethany.
165. Name three Bible cities that begin with C.
166. Locate (1) Cana; (2) Capernaum; (3) Corinth.
167. Name three Bible cities that begin with J.
168. Locate (1) Jerusalem; (2) Jericho; (3) Joppa.
169. Name three Bible cities that begin with T.
170. Locate (1) Tyre; (2) Tarsus; (3) Troas.
171. Name two Bible lands in the continent of Asia.
172. Name two Bible lands in the continent of Europe.
173. Name one Bible land in the continent of Africa.
174. In what province of Asia Minor is Ephesus?
175. Give four names applied to the Holy Land.
176. What State compares in shape and size to the Holy Land?
177. Name an important city situated near each of the following rivers: (1) Nile; (2) Euphrates; (3) Jordan; (4) Tigris.
178. Name the lake on which Jesus walked.
179. Name the mountain on which Jesus was transfigured.
180. Name the mountain on which the temple stood.
181. Name the mountain from which Jesus ascended.
182. What city was the residence of Simon the tanner?
183. Name the place from which Moses sent twelve spies into Canaan.
184. Name the five political divisions of Palestine in the time of Christ.
185. Name the five natural divisions of Palestine.

PART VI. FIVE LESSONS ON OLD TESTAMENT INSTITUTIONS.

186. Name the four great institutions of worship in the Old Testament.
187. What was the purpose of the altar?
188. Name the three parts of the tabernacle.
189. What furnishings were in the court?
190. What furnishings were in the Holy Place?
191. What was in the Holy of Holies? (395)
192. Give the typical meaning of the following: (1) Court; (2) Holy Place; (3) Holy of Holies; (4) Altar of Burnt-offerings; (5) Laver; (6) Golden Candlestick; (7) Table of Showbread; (8) Altar of Incense.
193. Name the five kinds of offerings.
194. Of what were each of the five offerings an expression?
195. Who built the first temple?
196. When was Solomon's temple destroyed?
197. Who rebuilt Solomon's temple?

198. What became of Zerubbabel's temple?
199. Who rebuilt Zerubbabel's temple?
200. What temple stood during Christ's time?
201. In what period of Old Testament history was (I) the first temple built? (2) The second?   (3) The third?
202. Name the six departments of the temple.
203. During what captivity did the synagogue rise?
204. With what person do we associate the origin of the synagogue?
205. What two ways the synagogue aided in preparing the world for Christ?

206. Name the three great feasts of the Jews.
207. What did the Passover commemorate?
208. What did Pentecost commemorate?
209. What did the Feast of the Tabernacles commemorate?
210. Name the three lesser feasts of the Jews.
211. What was the only fast day required by the Jewish law?
212. What special thing was done on the Day of Atonement?

PART VII. THE BIBLE SCHOOL.

213. Who put the modern Sunday-school "on the market"? When?
214. When was the International Lesson system inaugurated?
215. Name the seven departments of a well-organized Bible school.
216. About how many Bible-school conventions are annually held in North America?
217. When did the International Sunday-school Association elect a teacher-training superintendent?
218. Define the Bible school.
219. What is the relation of the Bible school to all other organizations of the church?
220. Name four things that the church needs that the Bible school furnishes.

221. Who should constitute the Home Department?
222. Give three benefits of the Home Department.
223. Define the graded Bible school.
224. Name the seven essentials of the graded school.
225. Name one great value of the graded Bible school.
226. Through supplemental work, what four things at least should be taught?

227. How do graded supplemental lessons aid in grading a school?

PART VIII. THE TEACHER AND HIS WORK.

228. Name the first and chief qualifications of the teacher.
229. Name two ways in which he must be a Christian.
230. Name two ways in which a teacher must be a student.
231. Name three ways in which a teacher must be a friend.
232. Name three elements in the teacher's preparation of himself.
233. Name three steps in the preparation of a lesson.
234. Name the seven elements found in every lesson.
235. Tell how to secure home study.
236. What is the difference between principles and methods in teaching?

237. Name six principles in teaching.
238. Name seven week-day influences surrounding the scholars.
239. Name the five formal steps in teaching.
240. Upon what law of the mind is testing based?
241. What is the difference between testing and presentation.
242. Name two ways by which association may be made.
243. Define generalization.
244. What is the object of the application?
245. What three M's should a teacher know?
246. Define "attention."
247. Name five methods of securing attention.

248. Define "sensation."
249. Define "perception."
250. Define "apperception.
251. Name the five senses.
252. Define "memory."
253. Define "imagination."
254. Define "feelings."
255. Define the "will."
256. Define "habit."
257. Name the two general methods of teaching.
258. What is the "question" method often called?
259. Name three kinds of questions to be used with care.
260. Name five kinds of questions to be asked.
261. Name five uses of questions.
262. Name three kinds of questions that should not be asked.
263. Upon what law of teaching are illustrations based?
264. Name two kinds of illustrations.
265. Name three characteristics of a good illustration.
266. Name four uses of illustrations.
267. Name three ways of securing illustrations.
268. What is the best book on illustrations?

PART IX. THE PUPIL.

269. Name the seven periods in life and give the approximate ages covered by each.
270. Name four methods in studying the child.
271. Name four general characteristics of children.
272. Give the twofold classification of temperament.
273. Name five characteristics of the beginners.
274. Name five things that we owe the beginners.
275. Name five characteristics of the primary pupils.
276. What two senses are most used by the primary teacher?
277. Name five things that we owe the primary children.
278. Name five characteristics of the junior pupils.
279. Name five things that we owe the juniors.
280. What is manual work?
281. Define "adolescence."
282. Name five characteristics of the intermediates.
283. Name five things that we owe the intermediates.
284. Into what two divisions does the adult department naturally fall?
285. Name five characteristics of the young people.
286. Name five characteristics of the older adults.
287. Name three things that we owe the young people.
288. Name three things that we owe the older adults.
289. What is an organized class?

NOTE.—Brief answers to these questions that will make possible concert class drills, Bible drill matches, etc., may be found in a book called "Bible Drills." This book contains over 700 questions and answers. Price, 25 cents, manilla binding; 40 cents, cloth binding; manilla binding, in lots of one dozen or more, 20 cents each. Address all orders to the Standard Publishing Co., Cincinnati, O.

ANSWERS TO DRILL QUESTIONS

These answers are made brief to aid the memory. **Fuller answers may** be found in the various lessons.

PART I. THE BIBLE AND ITS BOOKS.

1. Book.
2. (1) Word of God; (2) Scriptures.
3. Old Testament and New Testament.
4. Thirty-nine.
5. Twenty-seven.
6. Sixty-six.
7. Law, History, Devotion, Major Prophets, Minor Prophets.
8. Five, twelve, five, five, twelve.
9. Genesis, Exodus, Leviticus, Numbers, Deuteronomy.
10. Joshua, Judges, Ruth, 1 Samuel, 2 Samuel, 1 Kings, 2 Kings, 1 Chronicles, 2 Chronicles, Ezra, Nehemiah, Esther.
11. Job, Psalms, Proverbs, Ecclesiastes, Song of Solomon.
12. Isaiah, Jeremiah, Lamentations, Ezekiel, Daniel.
13. Hosea, Joel, Amos, Obadiah, Jonah, Micah, Nahum, Habakkuk, Zephaniah, Haggai, Zechariah, Malachi.
14. Biography, History, Special Letters, General Letters, Prophecy.
15. Four, one, fourteen, seven, one.
16. Matthew, Mark, Luke, John.
17. Acts.
18. Romans, 1 Corinthians, 2 Corinthians, Galatians, Ephesians, Philippians, Colossians, 1 Thessalonians, 2 Thessalonians, 1 Timothy, 2 Timothy, Titus, Philemon, Hebrews.
19. James, 1 Peter, 2 Peter, 1 John, 2 John, 3 John, Jude.
20. Revelation.
21. Matthew.
22. Mark.
23. Luke and Acts.
24. John, 1 John, 2 John, 3 John, Revelation.
25. Paul.
26. (1) 1 Peter, 2 Peter; (2) James; (3) Jude.
27. Matthew, Mark, Luke.
28. Matthew, John.

PART II. EVIDENCES.

29. (1) Meets human needs; (2) Unity; (3) Superiority; (4) Influence; (5) Man unaided could not have produced it.
30. (1) Bible declares it; (2) He fulfilled prophecy; (3) No other **way** to explain the effect of his life; (4) His sinlessness; (5) His resurrection.

PART III. OLD TESTAMENT HISTORY.

31. Adam, Noah, Abraham, Joseph, Moses, Joshua, Gideon, Samuel, Saul, David, Solomon, Elijah, Isaiah, Jeremiah, Daniel, Nehemiah.
32. Cain.
33. Abel.
34. Shem, Ham, Japheth.
35. Lot was Abraham's nephew.
36. Reuben, Simeon, Levi, Judah, Issachar, Zebulon.
37. Joseph, Benjamin.
38. Dan, Naphtali.
39. Gad, Asher.
40. Egypt.
41. Nebo.
42. Joshua.
43. Rule of the Judges.
44. Samson.
45. Deborah.
46. Samuel.

47. Fifteen.
48. Saul.
49. Samuel.
50. David.
51. Samuel.
52. Solomon.
53. Solomon.
54. Israel.
55. Jeroboam.
56. Judah.
57. Rehoboam.
58. Probation, Preparation, Conquest, Power, Decline, Servitude.
59. From the creation to the deluge.
60. From the deluge to the Exodus.
61. From the Exodus to the coronation of Saul.
62. From the coronation of Saul to the division of the kingdom.
63. From the division of the kingdom to the Babylonian captivity.
64. From the Babylonian captivity to Christ.
65. Four.
66. Fall, Promise of Redemption, Deluge.
67. Dispersion, Journeys of Patriarchs, Experiences in Egypt.
68. Experiences in the Wilderness, Conquest of Canaan, Rule of the Judges.
69. Saul's Defeat, Ark Removed, Temple Built.
70. Chaldean Rule, Persian Rule, Greek Rule, Maccabean Liberty, Roman Rule.
71. Division, Decay.
72. Adam, Noah.
73. Abraham, Joseph.
74. Moses, Joshua, Gideon, Samuel.
75. Saul, David, Solomon.
76. Elijah, Isaiah, Jeremiah.
77. Daniel, Nehemiah, Zechariah, Ezra, Malachi.
78. (1) B. C. 721; (2) B. C. 587; (3) B. C. 536.
79. Moses.
80. Joshua.
81. Deborah, Gideon, Samson, Samuel.
82. With the fall of Samaria, B. C. 721.
83. Isaiah.
84. Jeremiah.
85. Cyrus.
86. Greek.
87. Judas Maccabeus.
88. Roman.
89. The same person.

PART IV. NEW TESTAMENT HISTORY.

90. (1) Life of Christ; (2) Beginnings of the Church; (3) Life of Paul.
91. (1) Preparation; (2) First Year; (3) Second Year; (4) Third Year; (5) Last Three Months; (6) Last Week; (7) Forty Days.
92. Birth, Flight, Return, Baptism, Temptation.
93. First Miracle, First Cleansing, Nicodemus, Woman of Samaria. Nobleman's son.
94. Calling Fishers, Sermon on the Mount, Widow's son, Lakeside Parables, Jairus' daughter.
95. Feeding five thousand, Syrophoenician's daughter, Peter's confession, Transfiguration, Good Samaritan.
96. Lazarus, Ten Lepers, Little Children, Rich young ruler, Zaccheus.
97. Mary's anointing, Triumphal entry, Ten virgins, Upper room, Crucifixion.
98. Appearance to two, Appearance to ten, Appearance to seven, Appearance to five hundred, Appearance to eleven.
99. See Answers 92-98, inclusive.
100. Bethlehem.
101. To Egypt, to escape Herod, who wanted to kill him.

102. Nazareth.
103. John the Baptist.
104. Jordan.
105. "This is my beloved Son, in whom I am well pleased."
106. Cana.
107. Two.
108. Nicodemus.
109. "Year of Obscurity."
110. Galilee.
111. Matthew.
112. Nain.
113. Capernaum.
114. "Year of Popularity."
115. Feeding the five thousand.
116. "Thou art Christ, the Son of the living God."
117. Matt. 16 : 16.
118. "This is my beloved Son, in whom I am well pleased; hear ye him."
119. Luke.
120. "Year of Opposition."
121. Zaccheus.
122. Sunday.
123. Jerusalem.
124. The Lord's Supper.
125. (1) First Year; (2) First Year; (3) Preparation; (4) Second Year; (5) Second Year; (6) Third Year; (7) Second Year; (8) Last Week; (9) Last Week; (10) Third Year; (11) Third Year; (12) Forty Days; (13) Last Week; (14) First Year.
126. Different answers may be given to this question. Six very important ones are John the Baptist, Luke, John, Peter, Paul and Stephen.
127. Nazareth, Capernaum, Bethany.
128. Joseph of Arimathea.
129. Nicodemus (John 19 : 38-42).
130. (1) Church at Jerusalem; (2) Church outside of Jerusalem.
131. On the day of Pentecost following the resurrection.
132. Cornelius.
133. All but John.
134. Ananias and Sapphira.
135. (1) Pentecost; (2) Persecution; (3) Hypocrites; (4) Deacons; (5) Stephen.
136. Philip, Peter, Paul.
137. (1) Student; (2) Persecutor; (3) Convert; (4) Missionary; (5) Author; (6) Prisoner.
138. Tarsus.
139. Jerusalem.
140. Gamaliel.
141. Stephen.
142. Paul.
143. Acts 9, 22, 26.
144. Three.
145. Barnabas, Silas, Luke.
146. Timothy.
147. Cæsarea, Rome.
148. Nero.
149. Patriarchal, Jewish, Christian.
150. (1) Adam to Moses; (2) Moses to Christ; (3) Christ to the present time.
151. Altar.
152. Tabernacle, Temple, Synagogue.
153. The church.

PART V. BIBLE GEOGRAPHY.

154. Nile, Euphrates, Jordan.
155. (1) In Egypt; (2) In the western part of Asia, east of Palestine; (3) In Palestine.
156. Mediterranean.

157. Persian.
158. Galilee.
159. Dead.
160. Red.
161. Sinai, Nebo, Carmel, Hermon, Olives.
162. (1) In the wilderness; (2) Near northern end of Dead Sea, east of the Jordan River; (3) Near the Mediterranean Sea, due west of the Lake of Galilee; (4) At the source of the Jordan, about forty miles above the Lake of Galilee; (5) In Judea near Jerusalem.
163. Babylon, Bethlehem, Bethany.
164. (1) In Chaldea; (2) In Judea; (3) In Judea.
165. Cana, Capernaum, Corinth.
166. (1) In Galilee; (2) In Galilee; (3) In Greece.
167. Jerusalem, Jericho, Joppa.
168. (1) In Judea; (2) In Judea; (3) In Judea.
169. Tyre, Tarsus, Troas.
170. (1) In Phœnicia; (2) In Cilicia; (3) In Mysia.
171. (1) Palestine; (2) Asia Minor.
172. (1) Macedonia; (2) Italy. Others may be mentioned.
173. Egypt.
174. Lydia.
175. (1) Canaan; (2) Israel; (3) Judea; (4) Palestine.
176. New Hampshire.
177. (1) Memphis; (2) Babylon; (3) Jericho; (4) Nineveh.
178. Galilee.
179. Hermon.
180. Moriah.
181. Mount of Olives.
182. Joppa.
183. Kadesh-barnea.
184. (1) Judea; (2) Samaria; (3) Galilee; (4) Perea; (5) Bashan.
185. (1) Maritime plain; (2) Foot-hills; (3) Mountain region; (4) Jordan valley; (5) Eastern tableland.

PART VI. LESSONS ON OLD TESTAMENT INSTITUTIONS.

186. Altar, Tabernacle, Temple, Synagogue.
187. The altar was "a meeting-place between God and man, involving a sacrifice for sin."
188. Court, Holy Place, Holy of Holies.
189. Altar of Burnt-offerings, Laver.
190. Golden Candlestick, Table of Showbread, Altar of Incense.
191. Ark of the Covenant.
192. (1) World; (2) Church; (3) Heaven; (4) Christ's sacrifice; (5) Christian baptism; (6) Bible; (7) Lord's Supper; (8) Prayer.
193. Sin, Burnt, Trespass, Meal, Peace.
194. (1) Sin—reconciliation; (2) Burnt—atonement; (3) Trespass—forgiveness; (4) Meal—thanksgiving; (5) Peace—communion.
195. Solomon.
196. B. C. 587.
197. Zerubbabel.
198. It became dilapidated.
199. Herod the Great.
200. Herod's temple.
201. (1) Power; (2) Servitude; (3) Herod's temple was begun in the period of Servitude, but was not finished until after the coming of Christ.
202. (1) Court of the Gentiles; (2) Sacred Inclosure; (3) Court of the Women; (4) Court of Israel; (5) Court of the Priests; (6) Temple Proper.
203. Babylon.
204. Ezra.
205. It furnished a place and a people.
206. Passover, Pentecost, Tabernacle.
207. The passing over of the death angel and the departure from Egypt.
208. Giving of the law at Mt. Sinai.
209. Life in the Wilderness.

210. Trumpets, Dedication, Purim.
211. Day of Atonement.
212. The high priest entered the Holy of Holies to sprinkle blood upon the mercy-seat of the ark of the covenant.

PART VII. THE BIBLE SCHOOL.

213. Robert Raikes in 1780.
214. 1873.
215. Cradle Roll, beginners', primary, junior, intermediate, adult, home.
216. 15,000.
217. W. C. Pearce in 1903.
218. The Bible school is the teaching service of the church to win souls to Christ and to train them in Christian service.
219. The Bible school lays the foundation upon which all other organizations of the church build.
220. (1) A department of education; (2) a workshop; (3) a place to develop Bible teachers; (4) an evangelizing agency.
221. Those who do not attend the regular school or belong to the Cradle Roll.
222. (1) Increases Bible study; (2) increases home religion; (3) increases Bible-school attendance.
223. The graded Bible school is one that fits the Bible to the scholar as he develops from year to year and period to period.
224. (1) Departments and grades; (2) Departments organized; (3) Enrollment secretary; (4) Adaptation of teachers; (5) Adaptation of lessons; (6) Supplemental lessons; (7) Regular promotion day.
225. Makes teaching definite.
226. (1) Memory passages fitted to each grade; (2) The names of the books of the Bible and their divisions; (3) Outlines of Old and New Testament history; (4) Outlines of Bible geography.
227. Supplemental lessons serve, in the main, as a basis for promotions and graduations.

PART VIII. THE TEACHER AND HIS WORK.

228. Christian.
229. (1) In purpose; (2) In practice.
230. (1) In teachableness; (2) In thoroughness.
231. (1) In sympathy; (2) In sacrifice; (3) In service.
232. (1) Prayer; (2) Study; (3) Conversation.
233. (1) Facts; (2) Facts for self; (3) Facts for scholars.
234. Places, persons, dates, doings, difficulties, doctrines, duties.
235. Assign it, expect it, call for it, commend it, use it.
236. Principles are the abiding foundations upon which all work is done, and methods are the plans of building in accordance with them.
237. (1) Put the new in an old setting; (2) Use words that are understood by the teacher and the scholar in the same sense; (3) Adapt the teaching to the needs of the scholar; (4) Secure co-operation; (5) The development of the subject must constantly present new points of interest; (6) Ideas must be repeated to be retained.
238. Home, school, street, reading, recreation, companions, occupation.
239. (1) Testing; (2) Presentation; (3) Association; (4) Generalization; (5) Application.
240. "The mind can receive new knowledge only through similar ideas already known."
241. "Testing" is finding the foundation and "presentation" is building thereon.
242. (1) Comparison; (2) Contrast.
243. Broad statement of truth deduced from facts under consideration.
244. Translate words into works.
245. Matter, Mind, Method.
246. Focused consciousness.
247. (1) Contact; (2) Curiosity; (3) Concreteness; (4) Co-operation; (5) Contagion.
248. An impression made upon the mind by an outside stimulus.
249. The recognition of a sensation.

250. The translation and interpretation of the new in terms of the old.
251. Taste, touch, smell, hearing, sight.
252. The power of the mind to retain, recall and recognize.
253. The picture-producing power of the mind.
254. Mental states of pleasure and pain.
255. Self-determining power of the mind.
256. Second nature.
257. (1) Lecture; (2) Question.
258. The Socratic method.
259. (1) Rhetorical; (2) Elliptical; (3) Yes and no.
260. (1) Clear; (2) Constructive; (3) Original; (4) Suggestive; (5) Spiritual.
261. (1) To awaken interest; (2) To aid the memory; (3) To test the scholar's knowledge; (4) To arouse the scholar's conscience; (5) To test the teacher's work.
262. (1) Foolish; (2) Catch; (3) Long-answered.
263. Proceed from the concrete to the abstract.
264. (1) Verbal; (2) Material.
265. (1) Must illustrate; (2) Not too much detail; (3) Intelligible.
266. (1) Attract attention; (2) Aid the memory; (3) Aid the understanding; (4) Mirror the life.
267. (1) Through observation; (2) Through speakers and teachers; (3) Through reading.
268. The Bible.

PART IX. THE PUPIL.

269. Cradle Roll, Beginners, Primary Proper, Junior, Intermediate, Young People, Older Adults. (1) Birth to three; (2) three to six; (3) six to nine; (4) nine to twelve; (5) twelve to sixteen; (6) sixteen to about twenty-five; (7) twenty-five to death.
270. (1) Watch his outward actions; (2) Imagine what we would do under such circumstances; (3) Study well-written books for and about children; (4) Listen to those who have made a special study of child nature.
271. (1) Restlessness; (2) Curiosity; (3) Play instinct; (4) Love for stories.
272. (1) Motor; (2) Sensory.
273. (1) Physical restlessness; (2) Uncontrolled imagination; (3) Inquisitiveness; (4) Can not read; (5) Play instinct.
274. (1) Separate room; (2) Suitable pictures; (3) Simple music; (4) Suitable chairs; (5) Suitable lessons.
275. (1) Beginning of school age; (2) Imitation; (3) Desire for certainty; (4) Intense activity; (5) Limited vocabulary.
276. (1) Seeing; (2) Hearing.
277. (1) Suitable room; (2) Graded department; (3) Suitable chairs; (4) Well-planned programs; (5) Suitable working tools.
278. (1) Reading period; (2) Inquisitive period; (3) Friendly period; (4) Memory period; (5) Habit-forming period.
279. (1) Bibles; (2) Tables for manual work; (3) Graded supplemental work; (4) Suitable reading; (5) Adaptation of lessons.
280. Work that the pupils may do by hand, such as the making of outline maps, scrap-books, the writing of biographies of men, etc.
281. Adolescence is the period of human life that lies between puberty and the time at which the body acquires full development.
282. (1) Rapid physical growth; (2) Keen sense of humor; (3) Love for the thrilling; (4) Hero worship; (5) Fighting.
283. (1) Intermediate teachers; (2) Suitable reading; (3) Suitable supplemental lessons; (4) Organized classes; (5) Teachers of the same sex.
284. (1) Young people; (2) Older adults.
285. (1) Investigative; (2) Homing instinct; (3) Sensitive to public opinion; (4) Strong sense of honor; (5) Life of joy.
286. (1) Patriotism; (2) Reflective powers; (3) Love of quiet conversation; (4) Love for humanity; (5) Executive ability.
287. (1) Organized classes; (2) Proper religious atmosphere; (3) Training-class.

288. (1) Capable teachers; (2) Organized classes; (3) An opportunity for adequate Christian service.

289. One that has a teacher, president, vice-president, secretary, treasurer, and at least three committees—Social, Devotional, Lookout.*

---

*NOTE.—This is the minimum of an organized class. Other officers and committees may be added according to the desire of the local class.

"What's the Answer?"

Charley met his friend James upon the street and told him that he had been fishing. "How many fish did you catch?" asked James.

Charley replied: "If to the number of the books of the Old Testament you add the number of the books in the New Testament; multiply that by the number of apostles that were present at the transfiguration; divide by the number of the books written by Luke; subtract the number of times the Israelites marched around Jericho; multiply by the number of pieces of silver Judas received for betraying Christ; divide by the number of spies Moses sent into Canaan; add the number of letters in the name of the city in which a man climbed up a tree to see Christ; divide by the number of apostles that were called the 'sons of thunder,' the answer will be the number of fish I caught." The answer to this question is 111.

This is one of the twenty-six interesting Bible problems found in a book called "What's the Answer?" This book may be secured from the Standard Publishing Company, Cincinnati, O., for 25 cents, postpaid. Special price in quantities.

What One of These Problems Did

One of these problems was given to a boy who went home very enthusiastic about finding the answer. He got along all right until he came to the name of the city in which a man climbed up a tree to see Christ. He went to his mother and asked her if she knew what the man's name was and in what city he lived. She did not want to say that she did not know, so she put him off until the next day. In the meantime, she called up her preacher, and he said he would look it up. The boy then went the next day to school and asked his public-school teacher. She said the incident was very familiar to her, but she would tell him the next day just where to find it. This public-school teacher went home and asked her mother, who said she had heard of the story, but could not locate it. This mother also called up her preacher, and that preacher said he would look it up. From this one question at least two mothers, one public school teacher and two preachers were taught that Zaccheus was the man that climbed up a tree to see Christ, and that he lived in Jericho. Get these puzzle problems and try them in your class.

BIBLE DRILLS

BY

HERBERT MONINGER

A BOOK containing 750 questions and answers, on the Bible and Bible-school work, for use in Bible contests, general supplemental work, etc. This was the book used at the great Bible match between Cleveland and Cincinnati. "Of course you want one."

WAYS OF USING THIS BOOK

1. Follow the plan of the old-fashioned "spelling-bee." Appoint captains to choose up two sides. After this plan has been followed for awhile, let one class in the school challenge another class; or, let the men have a "Bible Drill-down" against the women. After a sufficient number have been drilled in one school, let that school challenge another one for a "Bible Drill Match," to be held at a time and place agreed upon by the two schools. We have tried this plan often, and always with encouraging results.

2. Drill the class in concert upon a chosen number of these questions; then, on some special occasion, let this class give a twenty-minute concert drill in the presence of the audience. On one occasion it was our privilege to conduct a twenty-minute Bible drill in which eight hundred people participated. The enthusiasm was intense and the effect most wholesome.

3. Arrange for a Bible drill at your township, county or State convention. A pleasant contest could be arranged where a number of classes participated, and a suitable recognition could be given to the classes doing the best work.

4. Have small groups of people meet in various homes to drill each other on these questions. Do not be afraid of drilling too much. These facts will be a part of your life's treasures, so grasp them tight.

5. These drill questions may be used in your Junior Christian Endeavor societies.

6. Many will feel it advantageous to use the drill questions for general supplemental work in the Bible school.

When any of the above suggestions are followed, each person participating should have a book.

These seven hundred questions and answers may be used in connection with any system of Bible study. Some of them are easy enough for the boys and girls, while others are plenty hard enough for the most studious adults. The person who can answer these drill questions will have a firm grasp upon the general facts of the Bible.

PRICES:

Manila, single copy, 25c.; per dozen, $2.40
Cloth, single copy, 40c.; per dozen, $4.20

THE STANDARD PUBLISHING COMPANY

BOX 764, CINCINNATI, O.